IMMANUEL BIRMELIN

My
Guinea Pig

BARRON'S

CONTENTS

1 Typical Guinea Pig

2 How Guinea Pigs Like to Live

Welcome Home

Providing a Nutritious, Delicious Diet

5 Grooming and Health Care

6 Activities and Wellness

Family Planning

What to Do When There Are Problems

Appendix

Typical Guinea Pig

They are good-natured, don't scratch or bite, are easily tamed, and love to be petted—in short, ideal pets. However, guinea pigs also have certain requirements.

Meet the Guinea Pig

Where do these little rodents come from? How do they live? What can they do? All these questions are important if you want to give your guinea pigs the best possible care. Only if you know the answers will you be able to understand these animals and meet their needs.

The appearance of our guinea pigs has changed dramatically over the last thousand years. Once humans set about breeding them for their own purposes, the nondescript, grayish brown rodent of the wild was transformed into a chunky, colorful pet.

Guinea Pigs: Livestock as Well as Pets

Just recently scientists in Bolivia succeeded in breeding a guinea pig that weighs up to 10 pounds (4.5 kg); normally they weigh $1\frac{3}{4}$ to $2\frac{1}{4}$ pounds (800 to 1,000 g). This giant among guinea pigs reveals the true aim of the South Americans: They wanted an animal that tastes good and provides plenty of meat. This is nothing new, but has been the case since ancient times. The shared history of humans and guinea pigs goes back a long way. Early inhabitants of the Peruvian highlands began domesticating the little rodent around 4000 B.C. The wild animal became a pet. The Peruvians haven't lost their appetite for guinea pig; today they consume 65 million guinea pigs a year. In every farmers' market, the animals are pulled out of sacks and offered for sale. The

farmers keep them in pits in their homes, preferably near the hearth. There is nothing romantic about this; it's just part of everyday life in the country. However, different systems of husbandry are needed to produce about 17,000 tons of guinea pig meat. The little creatures are bred in large farms, similar to our cattle and pigs. Unlike their South American cousins, guinea pigs in Europe and North America are never used for food. Here they are children's beloved pets. When Spanish conquerors brought them back to Europe in the 16th century, they immediately won the hearts of the nobility. Since

Ever alert: ▶
Guinea pigs are
by no means lazy
or even boring
animals!

The wild Cavy (Cavia aperea) is one of three species from which the domestic guinea pig developed. The range of the genus Cavia extends from Colombia to Argentina.

then, they have continued to captivate us. Guinea pigs are among our most popular pets. Their wild ancestors, however, don't enjoy this much affection.

The Wild Ancestors

Wild guinea pigs, also called cavies, face a difficult struggle for survival in the wild, one for which they are superbly suited. They can withstand both heat and cold. Guinea pigs live in the temperate regions of Central and South America, from Colombia to Chile and Argentina. In the Andes they are found at altitudes up to 16,500 feet (5,000 m). They occur everywhere except the tropical lowlands and the coldest regions of the Andes. They are delicately built, quick, and with their coat well adapted to their environment. They become active at twilight and scurry along small trails from burrow to burrow. Their primary foods are tough grasses and herbaceous plants. They live in colonies

of 20 to 40 animals. Like almost all mammals, one male lays claim to several females and will defend them tooth and nail. The social structure of the wild cavy, like that of our domestic guinea pig, is the harem. But wild animals are different from house pets, as Christine Künzel of the University of Münster in Germany has demonstrated. The wild cousins are more aggressive, vigilant, and shy than domestic guinea pigs. In the domestic varieties, males engage in courtship behavior more frequently and social contact is more intense. Thanks to their grayish brown coat, wild cavies are so perfectly camouflaged that it's difficult to detect them in their natural habitat.

The discovery of a new species: Scientists at the University of Münster, under the direction of Professor Norbert Sachser, caused a scientific sensation: They discovered a new species of guinea pig. The discovery, as so often happens in science, was an accident. About six years ago, the scientists brought 12 rodents from the province of Cochabama in Bolivia. They intended to cross them with their yellow-toothed Cavies in an attempt to avoid problems caused by inbreeding. However, there were no offspring. It occurred to biologist Matthias Asher, who had observed the animals in the wild, that they behaved differently from other guinea pig species. The fathers played with their young instead of behaving aggressively toward them, and they were monogamous: One male lived with one female. This is highly unusual; only 3 to 5 percent of the 4,250 mammalian species worldwide are monogamous. Additional studies, including genetic analysis and comparisons of bones and teeth, confirmed it beyond a doubt: A new species of guinea pig had been discovered. The city of Münster should feel honored, because the "newcomer" was named after it: Münster Guinea Pig, scientific name Galea monasteriensis. This wild guinea pig weighs about 10 ounces (300 g) and is reddish gray.

Giant guinea pigs: One of the ancestors of our modern guinea pig was vastly different in size. When Marcelo Sanchez-Villagra of the University of Tübingen, Germany, found the skeleton of a monster cavy in Venezuela and explained that it was the ancestor of our guinea pigs, his announcement caused quite a stir. This giant was 10 feet (3 m) long, $4\frac{1}{4}$ feet (1.3 m) tall, and weighed 1,500 pounds (700 kg). It was the largest rodent that ever lived, as big as a buffalo. Why couldn't this monster survive? An animal this large naturally needs a great deal of food and lots of time to forage, so it can easily fall prey to larger predators. Speed is its only defense. The hoofed mammals of Africa are champion runners, and that ensures their survival. Based on the anatomy of *Phoberomys pattersoni*—that's the scientific name of this giant rodent—some scientists believe it was slow and there-

Life in the Herd

▶ 1 **Wild cavies,** in front of their shelter, survey their surroundings, alert to any sign of danger. Is the coast clear?

▶ 2 **The wild relatives** of our domestic guinea pigs live in colonies, where they form "harems." One male has several females, which he defends courageously against other cavies.

THE DIFFERENCES BETWEEN WILD CAVIES AND DOMESTIC GUINEA PIGS

	Wild Cavies	Domestic Guinea Pigs
Coat color	uniform, dark grayish brown	solid or patterned; many shades of brown, red, and black
Coat	short and smooth	short and smooth, but also long and smooth; rosettes
Body type	slender; head delicately pointed; thin legs, small feet; small, erect ears; grows up to 8 inches (20 cm) in length	plump; broad head and blunt nose; ears larger, many breeds have slightly drooping ears; grows up to 13 inches (33 cm) in length
Behavior	They get used to people but remain skittish; bite when threatened. They are fast and agile and can jump up to 2 feet (60 cm) high.	They are easy to tame and quickly lose their shyness. Domestic guinea pigs rarely bite and get along better with others of their kind; are not high jumpers.
Vocalizations	Purring is heard rarely, and then only softly. "Chirping," also called singing, sounds like the warning call of birds and is frequently heard. They chirp when they are alarmed and find themselves in a state of conflict.	Individual guinea pigs differ greatly in the type and frequency of their vocalizations. The socially dominant males "purr" frequently and loudly. "Chirping" is less often heard, but "cooing" and "chattering" and "squeaking" may be observed among housemates. Guinea pigs may squeal in anticipation of a meal, when handled improperly, or when injured.
Herd life	When the young males are sexually mature, their fathers bite at them and drive them away mercilessly. Females, on the other hand, remain in the herd, and the young females assume a subordinate position in the hierarchy.	Here the male offspring are not expelled from the herd. Over the course of their life, they attain a rank in the herd hierarchy. Domestic guinea pigs are basically less aggressive than their wild relatives.

fore eaten by larger predators while grazing.

Biological Fact Sheet

Skeleton: There are four toes on the front legs and three on the hind legs. The collarbone is rudimentary. Guinea pigs have no tail, although surprisingly they have six caudal vertebrae (usually associated with tails). Based on their gait and the anatomy of their limbs, guinea pigs represent a transitional form between plantigrades (animals that walk on the sole of the foot) and digitigrades (animals that walk on their toes). When walking, they put their weight on their toes, but when standing their weight is on the sole.

Skin glands: Guinea pigs have sweat glands and sebaceous glands on the pads of their feet, among other places. Glands important for communal life are the supracaudal gland, near the sacrum (hip area), and the perineal glands, found between the anus and the reproductive organs. The supracaudal gland of the adult male produces secretions that are important for group cohesion, territorial behavior, and recognition of individuals. The scents of the perineal glands are used for marking.

Teeth: Both the upper and lower jaws have the same number of teeth, two incisors, two premolars, and six molars, but no canines. The molars grow continuously at a rate of $\frac{1}{16}$ inch (1.2 to 1.5 mm) per week. Guinea pigs are born with a fully developed set of teeth. The replacement of baby teeth by adult teeth takes place in the womb.

Heart: The animal's heart weighs about $\frac{1}{16}$ ounce (2.1 g) and beats 230 to 380 times a minute.

Body temperature: 100–103.5°F (approx. 37.8 to 39.7°C).
Head-to-tail length: $8\frac{3}{4}$ to 13 inches (22 to 33 cm).
Body weight: $1\frac{3}{4}$ to $2\frac{1}{4}$ pounds (800 to 1,000 g).
Gastrointestinal tract: The stomach has a capacity of $\frac{2}{3}$ to 1 ounce (20 to 30 ml). The intestine has a total length of

> Guinea pigs recognize each other by their **scent** and by the sounds they make.

$7\frac{1}{3}$ to $8\frac{1}{4}$ feet (2.25 to 2.49 m). Vegetable matter is first broken down by microorganisms in the intestine and then eliminated from the body. The animals eat these soft droppings, called cecotropes, while they're resting. Nutrients are then absorbed when this material makes its second trip through

Yellow dental enamel protects the teeth from wear and tear caused by constant gnawing. ▶

the digestive tract, and the resulting droppings are hard and dry.

Determining the Sex

At first glance, males ("boars") and females ("sows") look almost identical. Upon closer inspection, though, you can easily recognize the testicles in adult males as two pouches near the anus (see

Quite simply because if you know how guinea pigs perceive their environment, you will understand them more easily and treat them better. Sensory organs are the link to the outside world, and this is perceived differently by each animal species. Pet owners usually underestimate the importance of the senses. However, my years of experience with animals have taught me just how important it is to know something about sensory organs when sharing a home with guinea pigs.

DID YOU KNOW THAT . . .

. . . guinea pigs were important in ritual practices?

For thousands of years, guinea pigs have had a mythological significance among the inhabitants of Peru. In the folk medicine of the Andean tribes, they are important sacrificial animals. Written records describe how the Incas offered their gods 1,000 white guinea pigs and 100 white llamas every July on the central plaza of Cuzco. This ritual sacrifice was believed to ensure a good harvest.

photo, page 55). You can even determine the sex of newborns ("pups") if you use the right trick. Hold the guinea pig belly-up and then press the abdomen gently with your finger. In males the penis will protrude and be clearly visible. Naturally, you can also do this with older animals if you want to make sure of the sex.

The Senses

Why is it important to know how guinea pigs hear, see, smell, and feel?

For years, guinea pigs were assumed to be untrainable. The conclusion drawn from this was both incorrect and unfair: Guinea pigs are sweet, but not very bright. When we started training guinea pigs to press green, red, and blue keys to determine if they can see colors, we discovered that they were startled by high-pitched sounds and suddenly stood stock-still.

That day it was impossible to carry out any more experiments with the animals. How did we discover this? One member of the team—a musical genius—could

Guinea pigs can hear quite well.
They don't like **loud noises**. That's why
you should always speak softly to them.

hear sounds up to about 21,000 hertz that were inaudible to the rest of us. He noticed that the guinea pigs were startled by high-pitched sounds and refused to cooperate. The consequence was obvious: We shielded our guinea pigs from this noise and promptly met with success.

With the Eyes of a Guinea Pig

Like all herbivores, guinea pigs have eyes on the sides of their head. This lateral position of the eyes gives them a wide field of vision and allows them to see objects beside as well as behind them. The visual angle in guinea pigs is about 340 degrees. This panoramic view ensures their survival in the wild, for without this ability, they would easily be seized by predators. However, panoramic vision has its price. Guinea pigs have difficulty with depth perception. That's not terribly important in the grasslands of South America, but dangers lie in wait for them in your home. Your pets find it difficult or impossible to judge heights. That's why you must be careful that your guinea pig doesn't fall off the table when he's romping around up there. On the other hand, the little rodents perceive the slightest movement, and that protects them from hungry enemies. A guinea pig wouldn't enjoy himself at the movies, though. For guinea pigs, a movie is just a series of flickering images. That's because his

eyes differentiate 33 images per second, whereas the best we're capable of is 22. For a long time, it was thought that they can't see colors, but that's not true. In our studies on behavior, we were able to show that they can differentiate between red, green, and blue. These results were confirmed by other scientists. American researchers, however, have found only two types of cones—namely those for red and for green—in the guinea pig retina. Although no one contests their ability to see colors, it is still not certain if they can actually perceive the color blue.

Guinea pigs can see colors. This green house demands a closer look!
▼

With the Ears of a Guinea Pig

Guinea pigs are among the "chatterboxes" of the animal world; vocalizations accompany many of their behaviors. Each of these vocal signals conveys very specific information. They let a guinea pig know how herd mates feel or what they expect. Cooing and chattering, they stay in constant contact with each other; males and females recognize each other by certain sounds, and the affectionate squeaking of the females puts the rowdy males in a more peaceful mood. No wonder, then, that guinea pigs hear well. They definitely hear sounds ranging from 125 to 33,000 hertz, and they can probably even hear frequencies as high as 40,000 or 50,000 hertz. Sounds in the ultrasonic range are inaudible to humans. Our auditory range lies between 20 and 20,000 hertz, so guinea pigs are superior to us in the upper region. Like us, though, they don't hear all sounds of the auditory spectrum equally well. Our hearing is most acute at 2,000 hertz, and we have

to speak more loudly to be understood at other frequencies. The guinea pig ear is most receptive to frequencies between 500 and 8,000 hertz. Guinea pigs are sensitive to noise, especially if they are suddenly exposed to high-frequency sounds. They stand as if rooted to the spot, but there is a metabolic storm going on inside their body. The heart begins to race and stress hormones are churned out. That's why you should avoid any sudden noise. Get your animals accustomed to background noises slowly and carefully. That's good for you as well as your animals.

With the Nose of a Guinea Pig

If you watch your guinea pig, you'll quickly discover that his nose is frequently busy. He sniffs every new object, and his partner most of all. Scent is an important means of communication among guinea pigs. To study the effect of certain scents on guinea pig behavior, these experiments were conducted:

▶ The genital area of a female guinea pig was covered with a bandage marked with the urine of a male guinea pig. A different male guinea pig was then placed in her enclosure. What do you think happened? In this case, the male sniffed the female's genital area, immediately recoiled,

◀ *The guinea pig lives in a world of scent, and his nose is constantly busy. He carefully sniffs everything new and unfamiliar. What marvelous smells out here in the garden!*

and began to make soft threatening sounds.

▸ In the next experiment, the female guinea pig's bandage was marked with her male partner's urine. Her male partner was placed in her enclosure with her. In this situation, the male didn't recognize his own urine, shied away, and threatened softly.

▸ The question remains: Is there something fundamentally repellent about the urine or is there a difference between the urine of males and that of females? To answer this question, a female guinea pig wore a bandage marked with the urine of another female. In this case, the male placed in her enclosure immediately pursued her and tried to mount her.

We might conclude that male urine repels males and female urine attracts males and inhibits aggression.

If an unfamiliar male enters an occupied territory, the two rivals can fight until they are ready to drop. Research suggests it is the scent and not the appearance that makes them aggressive. Within established groups of guinea pigs, straw from an unfamiliar cage was rubbed on one neutered male in the group. The dominant male in each group immediately began to purr at and threaten his companion. Luckily for the neutered males, the added scent dissipated quickly.

Although no careful scientific studies have determined how well guinea pigs perceive smell, guinea pigs' smell is said to be better than that of humans but not as good as that of dogs. Because guinea pigs learn to recognize you by your personal scent, you should minimize covering your scent with perfumes or cleaning products.

TEST

Is a guinea pig right for me?

Guinea pigs are more demanding than some people claim. Take this test to see if guinea pigs are the right pet for you.

	Yes	No
1. Are you prepared to keep two or more guinea pigs?	○	○
2. Do you have enough time to allow the animals plenty of out-of-cage exercise every day?	○	○
3. Can someone take care of your pets while you're on vacation?	○	○
4. Are you prepared to devote time to your guinea pigs every day?	○	○
5. Would you have a sick animal treated by the veterinarian, even if it was expensive?	○	○
6. Do you enjoy observing guinea pig behavior?	○	○
7. Will you give them fresh foods like vegetables, lettuce, and fruit?	○	○
8. Will you wash the food bowl and water bottle every day?	○	○
9. Will you make sure the cage is clean?	○	○
10. Will you provide your guinea pigs with a variety of activities so that they don't get bored?	○	○

ANSWERS: Ten "yes": An owner like this is every guinea pig's dream. The animals will be very happy with you. Eight "yes": Perhaps you can give more thought to your negative responses. Fewer than five "yes": Guinea pigs are not right for you.

The Sense of Taste

Herbivores are among the animals with the greatest number of taste buds. Cattle are out in front: A cow has about 25,000 taste buds, whereas a rabbit has 17,000, a cat has only 473, and a human has 9,000. This is astonishing, but it makes perfect sense biologically. Herbivores must be able to distinguish the many good varieties of grass and plants from the poisonous and immature ones. Guinea pigs, too, are faced with this problem. It's hard to believe, but these "eating machines" choose their food very carefully. Scientists have found that they like to drink slightly sweetened water, but avoid it if it's too sweet. They didn't drink bitter water. This is understandable with bitter foods, because poisonous plants often taste bitter.

TIP

The whiskers are important

Guinea pigs can find their way in the dark using their whiskers (tactile hairs). Unfortunately, this ability is limited in some breeds because their whiskers are shortened or curly. This is frequently the case in Teddy, British Rex, and Texel guinea pigs (see beginning on page 25).

The Sense of Touch

You can easily see the long, coarse hairs arranged around the mouth and nose. These are whiskers, also called tactile hairs, and they have a very specific function. They provide guinea pigs with information about their immediate environment. Just as we use our fingertips or tongue to identify the shape of an object, guinea pigs use their whiskers. But that's not all. Whiskers help the animals find their way at twilight or in the dark. As these hairs brush against objects, they convey spatial information. We do more or less the same thing: We stretch out our arms in the dark and feel our way with our hands as we move about a room. The guinea pigs have an easier time of it because of their tactile hairs. They have to, because in the wild the animals don't become active until twilight. When a guinea pig is running away from an enemy, his whiskers help him find openings he can slip through. That's why you should never cut off your guinea pig's whiskers!

Depth perception is no easy task for ▶
guinea pigs.

How Guinea Pigs Live

There are few species we know better than guinea pigs. Many scientists have found them fascinating and studied their behavior. I have been deeply impressed by zoologist and behavioral biologist Professor Norbert Sachser as well as by Sylvia Kaiser and her team because they found a new way to understand the inner world of our pets.

Hormones control behavior

Many of our guinea pigs' behaviors are accompanied by an increase or decrease of hormone levels in the blood. Stress, for example, produces an increase in the hormone cortisol (see right). How they feel also depends on hormones. Guinea pigs are happy only with a partner or, better yet, in a group. They are social creatures and are not guided by instincts alone. Many types of behavior, like threatening, fighting, and courtship, are genetically programmed. What these animals do with them, however, depends heavily on socialization. Guinea pigs learn how to handle stress when they are youngsters. Among males there is a clear social hierarchy and a firm pair bond with the females. This social structure reduces stress. If a new-comer who doesn't know the rules joins the group, there is a fight. The owner of the territory advances toward the intruder with legs spread wide like some cowboy hero, the fur on his neck bristling and his teeth chattering. He doesn't do this because he's afraid, but rather to demonstrate his strength.

Then he assumes a threat posture and lowers his testicles in a display of aggression. Now things can get nasty. If the intruder doesn't back down, a bloody battle can ensue. The outcome can be fatal if the cage is too small and the vanquished guinea pig can't escape. At best, the loser retreats to one corner of the cage and stays there quietly. From his external appearance, you'd never guess that his stress hormone levels have doubled. It's not uncommon for him to waste away and die within a few days without any external injuries. If there's enough room, the rival gets a mini-territory where he can remain undisturbed (see page 35).

In your home, introducing guinea pigs must be done carefully. Provide a large space for the pigs to greet each other and hiding places should one

A Stranger Visits

▶ **1** **Mistrustfully,** the guinea pig eyes a stranger. She's still afraid to approach the intruder.

▶ **2** **Guinea pigs sniff** unfamiliar animals, particularly along the cheeks and under the chin.

▶ **3** **The nose knows** if the stranger is a male or a female. This is an encounter between two females.

need to get away. Consider separating the newcomer by a screen so that he can be seen and smelled but not reached. Watch the animals' behavior to determine when the introduction can move forward. When the guinea pigs seem tolerant of one another, allow supervised interaction as well as hiding places. Should the guinea pigs begin to fight, separate them, but do so carefully. This is one time they are likely to bite. If, over time, a guinea pig is not accepted in the group, he must be housed separately.

And why is the intact group so important for guinea pigs? It's quite simple: When danger threatens the group, the individual finds support in stable pair bonds. The animals can depend on each other, and that makes them peaceful. This is the key to reproductive success. In many species, overpopulation can have a boomerang effect. The animals no longer reproduce as often, and they begin to quarrel. This is not the case with guinea pigs.

In small groups, the male guinea pig always dominates. He is the absolute boss and defends his female. In large groups, on the other hand, the territory of the previous boss is divided up. This yields small territories in which the males protect their females. Guinea pigs have no problem accepting and respecting the position of others in the herd.

Gaining experience

During puberty, male guinea pigs learn how to deal with their position as a dominant or subordinate animal in the herd later on. However, this presupposes that they had the opportunity to test their strength against older, experienced males. This is how they learn the rules of the colony. There is no difference between the stress hormones of dominant animals and those of the subordinates. It all depends on how an animal accepts its rank. Being subordinate doesn't have to be bad; it's possible to be content with a lower rank. This attitude just has to be learned. Experiences

with others play an important role among guinea pigs and should not be underestimated by owners.

A fine example illustrates this: Males that grew up in one herd and were placed in an unfamiliar group for 20 days showed something surprising. In the first few days, they investigated their new surroundings and demonstrated absolutely no interest in the females. All went well because they didn't incur the wrath of the other males. Instead of being attacked, they were able to integrate themselves gradually into the group and even climb the social ladder.

Male guinea pigs that grew up alone and were later placed in a group fared worse. They lost weight and, although they had no external injuries, some died. They couldn't cope with the frequent threats and fights. Their hormones rebelled. And how did the other sex do? Females have an easier time getting used to a new herd, regardless of their upbringing.

The Intact "Family"

The researchers at the University of Münster recently found a new piece to the puzzle of guinea pig behavior. The pups of pregnant mothers that live in a stable environment behave differently from those of mothers in an unstable environment. In the stable environment, mothers lived permanently with one male and five females. To create an unstable environment, among other

TIP

Guinea pig companions help

Guinea pigs are very susceptible to stress. Studies have shown that the little rodents can manage stress much better if they live with others of their kind. It helps them deal with unfamiliar and unexpected situations. This is yet another argument against keeping just one guinea pig!

Guinea pigs are by nature
herd animals. In their native South
America, they live together in colonies.

groups, two females from different groups were switched every third day.

This seemingly minor change had major consequences. The daughters of mothers in an unstable environment displayed more masculine behavior. The male hormone testosterone was clearly elevated in the daughters, whereas the sons remained more immature. The herd life of these sensitive little creatures is fascinating, but by no means simple. That's why the composition of the group is so important.

Guinea pig companions are important

The wild relatives of our guinea pigs are herd animals. The need for others of their kind is written in their genes. The same is true of our domestic guinea pigs. If guinea pigs are moved from familiar surroundings to a sparsely furnished cage, stress hormone levels increase dramatically if the animal has

───────────

Whoever finds the apple first can dig right in.

to deal with the situation alone. If there are two guinea pigs, the rise in stress hormones is considerably less. Although a guinea pig may indeed look "cool" on the outside, his heart begins to beat faster in the new environment, and this agitated state lasts for 30 minutes. As one of a pair, his heart rate returns to normal after three minutes. Figures say it all. Stress lasts ten times as long in a solitary guinea pig as in a pair. Furthermore, an animal kept by itself has no partner for cooing, squealing, and purring. Without someone to "talk" to, life is lonely and boring, not just for us humans, but for guinea pigs, too.

Keeping a pair: The partners usually get along well. There are no fights and threats. The only problem is the offspring (see page 109).

Keeping females: Several females can be kept together without difficulty. However, aggression in a group like this is somewhat greater than in a herd with one male and several females. The females do quarrel with each other from time to time.

Keeping males: Two males are compatible. However, they need plenty of space in order to stay out of each other's way. During puberty, at about two to three months of age, they may fight to establish dominance, but this is usually not dangerous. If the squabbling gets too violent, then separate the two for a while.

Harmony will usually return. An older and a younger male cause the fewest problems. The "old man" is the dominant one.

However, I would advise against keeping several males. The danger that they won't get along is too great. A group like this is certainly fascinating to observe, though. Norbert Sachser discovered, for example, that some of the

together peaceably and everyone in the group learns to play by the rules.

On the other hand, a herd composed of a few males and many females is not a good idea. This usually leads to violent squabbles or even bloody battles.

DID YOU KNOW THAT . . .

. . . guinea pigs and rabbits may or may not be compatible?

It's very tempting to keep these two adorable animals together, but it's not a good idea. If you were to ask the guinea pigs which they would prefer as a companion—a rabbit or another guinea pig—the answer would be clear. Scientific studies have demonstrated this conclusively. Guinea pigs were permitted to choose between rabbits and other guinea pigs. The result left no doubt. They naturally chose their own kind. This comes as no surprise because rabbits and guinea pigs have, among other things, completely different circadian rhythms and they speak different languages. Another problem can develop, too. In the absence of other rabbits, a male rabbit will regard the guinea pig as a sexual partner and constantly attempt to mount it, or else the rabbit will pursue the guinea pig in the confines of the cage and bite it. This is pure stress for the guinea pig. Another significant concern is the possible transmission of *Bordetella* to the guinea pig, which can result in a potentially fatal pneumonia. Individual risks and housing situations must be assessed and, preferably, discussed with a veterinarian.

animals in an all-male group displayed female behavior. These "pseudo-females," as he calls them, were even courted enthusiastically by the other males. Nevertheless, this type of husbandry is not desirable.

Tip: Several males and females is the ideal guinea pig group because dominant and subordinate animals live

Behavior and Body Language

People who relate well to their fellow creatures and bond with them are usually guaranteed to do a good job keeping pets. A prerequisite for bonding with animals is to understand them and respect their special needs.

MY PET

Can guinea pigs see colors?

Place two food bowls on the floor 3 feet (approximately 1 m) apart. Take two pieces of cardboard measuring 2 × 4 inches (5 × 10 cm), one painted green and the other blue, and stand each one up behind a bowl (folded so that it remains upright.)

The test begins:

Place pelleted food in the bowl with the blue cardboard. The other bowl remains empty. Release a hungry guinea pig 3 feet (approximately 1 m) away and equidistant from both bowls. After a few trials (ten to fifteen), the pig will likely learn which bowl contains the food. To see if the pig recognizes the blue board, begin to place the blue board randomly behind empty bowls at each additional trial. Does the guinea pig continue to approach the blue board to look for food? To continue the association, reward the pig with food when he goes to the blue board first. This experiment can be repeated using different colors. How many colors can your pig recognize?

My test results:

Guinea pigs make it simple: Their behavior and their body language are easy to understand, even for us humans. **Threats:** When a guinea pig is feeling aggressive, the hair on the nape of his neck bristles if he is mildly irritated; if he's extremely annoyed, the hair stands on end all over his back, flanks, and cheeks. At the same time, he chatters his teeth loudly. Males display their testicles and circle their adversary. The guinea pig reinforces his intimidation tactics with his voice. He "purrs," making a sound like a drawn-out "br br br." **Treading:** When treading, the guinea pig puts more weight on his front legs and lifts first one hind leg, then the other. In the process, his hindquarters sway back and forth. The more subordinate a male and the more inclined he is to run away, the higher he lifts his feet and the more he swings his hindquarters. Guinea pigs tread when they want to intimidate an adversary.

Freezing: Frightened animals remain absolutely motionless, looking as if they're "frozen." Females and youngsters often freeze in response to an unfamiliar disturbance (noise of airplanes flying overhead, slamming doors). Lower-ranking males freeze when the dominant male approaches.

Urine spraying: A female guinea pig defends herself against a pushy suitor with a well-aimed jet of urine. She suddenly lifts her hindquarters as far as possible and shoots a jet of urine almost horizontally toward the rear. Females can spray their urine up to a distance of 12 inches (30 cm).

Rumba: The way male guinea pigs court the females calls to mind the dance steps of the Latin American rumba. The suitor circles his lady in slow motion and purrs.

Yawning: If a guinea pig yawns, he isn't tired, but rather has lost and is admitting defeat. The loser of a fight yawns at the victor and thus indicates his subordinate position.

Jumping: Just like human children, playful young guinea pigs jump for joy. And as with humans, the others follow suit.

Squealing: This is a long, piercing whistle and seldom fails to have the desired effect on humans. The animal begs for food this way.

Screaming: Guinea pigs make a loud, long-drawn-out cry when they are terrified or in pain.

Whistling: This long, soft, high-pitched sound is the distress call of abandoned youngsters.

Purring: Male guinea pigs make this deep rumbling sound with short trills when they threaten and mate.

Order, Please! Systematics

Given the multitude of plant and animal species on earth, it's obvious that they need to be organized somehow. Otherwise there would be chaos and people would never know what they were talking about. To that end, science has developed a system of nomenclature so that everyone—regardless of

nationality—knows precisely which animal or plant species is being discussed. Each of them knows that *Cavia aperea f. porcellus* is the domestic guinea pig. The scientific names are usually derived from Latin or Greek. We owe

Something's in the air. Is it the tasty leaf, or was another guinea pig in the neighborhood?

this ingenious system of classification to the Swedish naturalist Carl Linnaeus.

However, this taxonomic system is not an arbitrary creation; rather it is based on the fact that complex living organisms evolved from simpler creatures. As such, this classification is also an expression of natural relationships. The taxonomic description of the guinea pig reads as follows:

Class: Mammalia (mammals)
Order: Rodentia (rodents)
Family: Caviidae (cavies and their relatives)
Species: *Cavia aperea* (Wild Cavy)
Species: *Cavia aperea f. porcellus* (Domestic Guinea Pig).
The guinea pig is descended from the Wild Cavy (*Cavia aperea*), as indicated by the addition of *"forma domestica"* or *"forma porcellus"* to the scientific name.

Housing guinea pigs with parakeets is not a problem, provided you keep an eye on them.

▼

Guinea Pig Breeds

Guinea pigs come in an endless variety of colors as well as various coat lengths and textures. Making a choice can be overwhelming. On the following pages, you'll find a small selection of breeds.

Over time, the selective breeding of guinea pigs has led to the development of animals differing widely in coat color and type.

The Breed Standards

The color spectrum extends from pure white albinos with red eyes to pitch-black animals. The array of markings and coat textures is impressive. There are long-haired guinea pigs like the Peruvian; Abyssinian guinea pigs with whorls of hair called rosettes; and, of course, smooth-coated animals. The breeds differ in characteristics of body type, coat color, and coat type. These characteristics are set down in a breed standard. It forms the basis for breeding and sets out the criteria by which a guinea pig is selected as a champion at a show. The German, Austrian, and Swiss judges use the Dutch standard, and in the United States, judges follow the guidelines of the American Cavy Breeders Association (ACBA). The body type in all races should correspond to a specific standard. The "beauties" have a short and stocky ("cobby") body with sturdy hindquarters. The legs should be sturdy and straight. The head should appear broad, and the size of the head and distance between the eyes and ears should be well proportioned. The eyes should be round and clear. The hairless ears droop and have a slight wave in the middle ("rose-petal ears"). Other characteristics of beauty and good breeding include a rounded muzzle ("Roman nose") and well-developed cheeks. The weight of the animals can range from 25 to 42 ounces (700 to 1,200 g) for females and 25 to 63 ounces (700 to 1,800 g) for males.

In addition to the American and Dutch standards, there is also an English standard. The primary differences among these standards lie in the colors and the coat types of the guinea pigs.

TIP

Health problems

Give careful consideration to whether you want to have purebred guinea pigs that conform precisely to a breed standard. The round head and short muzzle much desired by breeders often leads to severe respiratory and dental problems in the animals. In addition, these animals suffer from heavy ocular discharge.

Portraits of
Breeds at a Glance

◀ Young Agouti Guinea Pig

This youngster's color is agouti, also known as wild-colored; in coloration, at least, he resembles his wild ancestors. The typical smooth-coated guinea pig has a rounded Roman nose, and the body is the same width from the shoulders to the hips. All guinea pigs have four toes on the front feet and three on the hind feet.

Adult Agouti ▶
Guinea Pig

Smooth-coated American guinea pigs come in a wide variety of colors. In all of them, the hair is about 1 inch (3 cm) long, lies close to the body, and has neither whorls nor waves. This agouti-colored animal is easy to distinguish from its wild relatives: In contrast to them, it has drooping rose-petal-shaped ears.

▲
Tricolor
This animal has a tricolor pattern. If the patches are sharply demarcated, almost like a checkerboard, the pattern is called tortoiseshell.

▲
Agouti and White Guinea Pig
The coat of smooth-coated guinea pigs is easy to groom and doesn't get soiled quickly, which is why they are especially suitable for beginners. This interesting silver agouti and white animal has ears with the common "rose-petal" shape, an intermediate form between erect and drooping ears.

Red and White ▶
This is not a genuine Dutch guinea pig—that's the name for a pattern consisting of a colored head with a white blaze and colored hindquarters—but she is still a pretty animal! Markings come in all colors, but not all meet the breed standard.

▲
Black and White
In this bicolor American guinea pig, beautiful markings like these black "cheeks" appeared quite by accident.

Satin Guinea Pig

This red American Satin guinea pig has a fine, lustrous coat. The special sheen is caused by the fact that the hair shafts are hollow and so reflect the light differently.

▲
Satin Guinea Pig

Unfortunately, this breed is often rather skittish and requires especially gentle care.

Teddy Guinea Pig ▶

This is one of the most popular breeds. The coat is characterized by its kinkiness and the absence of guard hairs. The hair is erect all over the body as if standing on end. Even the whiskers on the muzzle can be curly. The belly fur is somewhat thinner and shorter.

▲
Abyssinian Guinea Pig

Characteristics of this breed are long, harsh hair up to $1\frac{1}{2}$ inches (3.5 cm) in length and 8 to 12 rosettes distributed over the body.

▲
Tricolor Abyssinian Guinea Pig

Tricolor Abyssinian guinea pigs are extremely popular. This animal and the one on the lower right have a colorful mixture of white, black, and brown hairs. The coat of this breed feels coarse and firm. The rosettes give the animal a comical appearance.

Cream ▶

Abyssinian guinea pigs are not easy to breed. This shaggy critter is an attractive cream variety with large erect ears.

▲
Marked

According to the breed standard, the rosettes should be distributed evenly over the body: one rosette on each shoulder, four on the saddle, two on the rump, and one on each hip.

◀ Silkie

Here is a beautiful, dark gray animal. Silkies, called Shelties in Europe, do not have rosettes; their silky hair falls to the back and sides and is short around the face. This breed is a variation of the Peruvian.

▲

Peruvian

Summer is especially hot for long-haired breeds, so be sure to provide some shade.

▲

Peruvian Guinea Pig

This red and white Peruvian guinea pig with its perky top-knot is absolutely captivating. Peruvians, formerly known as Angoras, have long hair and at least two rosettes.

▲

Peruvian

They have long hair, two rosettes on the rump, a part down the middle of the back, and sometimes soft silky bangs, called a "frontal."

Texel Guinea Pig ▶

This breed has ringlets: Their long curly coat is parted down the middle and falls like a train to both sides. The hair on the face is short. This breed was developed in the 1980s from Silkie and British Rex guinea pigs. Texels get their long hair without whorls from the Silkie and their kinky coat from the Rex. Beautiful hair like this demands special care!

White Crested

These two chocolate and cream White Crested guinea pigs can be recognized by their white crest, which is also called a crown. In Europe, this breed is known as the American Crested.
▼

▲

English Crested

In this smooth-coated breed, the crown is not white, but instead is the same color as the rest of the coat. Here is a pretty tricolor variety with a red crest. This European breed is not yet recognized by the ACBA.

31

How Guinea Pigs Like to Live

No question about it—the companionship of other guinea pigs comes first. But a roomy cage and an exercise area with plenty of activities are also important for their well-being.

A Cozy Home for Your Guinea Pigs

It is easy to put yourself in your guinea pigs' place when it comes to housing. Would you like to live in an uncomfortable home? Of course not! That's why it's important to make a cozy home for your guinea pigs, too.

The well-being of our guinea pigs naturally depends on many things, including the size of the cage and how it's furnished. It's not much different for us humans—as we say, "My home is my castle." Nevertheless, there is one major difference. Guinea pigs are not individualists like us. If the cage meets certain standards, then our four-legged friends are happy. Luckily, there are many good suggestions that have been tested scientifically and proved in practice.

The Right Location for the Guinea Pig Cage

Light and shade. Find a place with both sun and shade. One part of the cage should always be shaded so that the animals can choose freely. Caution! Guinea pigs can't tolerate too much sunlight and heat; they can suffer heat-stroke, which can be fatal (see page 92). This means the windowsill is not a suitable spot for the cage.

A quiet place. Put the cage in a quiet, well-lit, draft-free location. The usual background noises don't bother guinea pigs, but high-frequency sounds can make them panic. More than one guinea pig has been injured severely by a frantic attempt to escape it.

An elevated place. Whether the cage is on the floor or on a small table is up to you. The advantage of a table is that you can watch your guinea pigs at eye level and they aren't likely to be disturbed by other house pets. A dog's snout in the cage can really frighten them. My little herd has grown accustomed to my German shepherd Teddy

A nice house and a friend—two requirements for making your guinea pig happy. ▶

2 **Wooden bridges** like this can be purchased at the pet store. The bridge is flexible, allowing the guinea pigs to climb easily in and out of the cage.

▼

1 **A hide box** is a must in every guinea pig cage. Wooden boxes are ideal, because the guinea pigs can chew on them, too.

3 **Variety** is good for guinea pigs. However, plastic objects are really not suitable for them. Choose natural materials, instead.

and he to them. They even greet him with a friendly gurgle. But that's certainly the exception and is partly because of Teddy, who has absolutely no hunting instinct.

Daytime creatures. Guinea pigs are not night owls like mice and rats. Two small herds were filmed for one week. At night, the guinea pigs mostly slept. In two- and three-hour cycles, they ran around, ate, drank, and sniffed at each other. Youngsters were not observed playing at night. In both groups, they were most active in the daytime. A bright, well-ventilated room for daytime activity should be provided.

Moderate temperature. The little rodents can't take the heat the way we can. Not too cold and not too hot is just

right. Temperatures between 59 and 68°F (15 and 20°C) are ideal. Slight variations are not harmful, and the guinea pigs tolerate them well. You definitely have to avoid drafts, though!

Moving the cage. Now here's a suggestion guaranteed to have true-blue guinea pig fans shaking their heads. If possible, shift the cage to another spot in the room every so often, or even move it into another room altogether for a while. Why? An interesting environment improves your guinea pigs' health and longevity. A change of scenery, viewed from the safety of their cage, provides enrichment for the guinea pigs. Animals that were snatched from their daily routine were much more curious and alert. No wonder, when you consider how the animals live in the wild. Instead of the "same old same old," there is constant change. Every day brings something new.

A Comfortable Cage for Your Guinea Pigs

As they say, the bigger the better. Of course, you're limited by the size of your pocketbook and, as a rule, the amount of space available. Guinea pigs can also be content with less if you use a few tricks.

Minimum cage size: For two guinea pigs, the cage should be at least 48 inches (120 cm) long, 32 inches (80 cm) wide, and 18 inches (45 cm) high. Think about it: The cage is the center of the guinea pigs' world. It's more than just a place to hide. It's both a cozy home and a playground.

For wild guinea pigs, searching for food is a strenuous job that keeps the lively rodents physically and mentally fit. Their caged relatives don't have to worry about their "daily bread." Consequently, many become lazy, fat, and listless. This problem can be solved by choosing the right cage and accessories.

The right cage

The cages at pet supply stores consist of a wire top and a bottom tray. This design has withstood the test of time because it is easy to handle and clean.

Cage wires: Galvanized or matte chrome-plated horizontal wires are best. The guinea pigs can support themselves on the wires with their front paws and see what's going on outside their cage. I advise against plastic-coated wires because there is a danger that

the little rodents will chew on them. Make sure that the plastic tray is no more than about 6 inches (16 cm) deep; otherwise the animals will feel cut off from their surroundings, and this makes them lethargic. Zoos have been making this foolish mistake for years. To avoid ugly cage bars, they stuck the animals in pits, much to the creatures' detriment. Your guinea pigs should have it better and should be able to see what's going on around them. Not only does this stimulate curiosity, but it also protects them from surprises and avoids negative stress and panic. In addition, low plastic trays prevent the buildup of heat and the development of unpleasant odors.

Connecting two cages: One cage is good, but two are much better. On the one hand, you can increase floor space this way; on the other, you can solve the annoying problem of overgrown toenails with a simple trick. Use wood shavings as the bedding in one cage (see page 38), and put garden soil interspersed with rocks in the other. A substrate like this will wear down the toenails well. Connect the two cages,

TIP

A hide box is a must

Guinea pigs are flight animals. In the wild, they don't defend themselves against enemies; instead, they run away. That's why it's so important for the cage or enclosure to have a hide box where your guinea pigs can retreat, even though as pets they have little to fear (see page 37).

perhaps by using a flexible ramp as a bridge (see photo, page 34).

Multilevel condo: Pet supply stores have been carrying multi-level condos for quite a while. These cages give the animals more room to move around because the floor space is doubled or even tripled, depending on the number of floors. This allows the animals to run

pages on the Internet, you can often find excellent suggestions for building cages like this as well as other types of housing carefully designed to meet the guinea pigs' needs (see Addresses and Literature, page 141).

DID YOU KNOW THAT . . .

. . . wild guinea pigs live the simple life?

The "wild ones" don't live as comfortably as our domestic guinea pigs with hideaways. Their homes are rather Spartan. Within their home range, the females have certain bushes or shelters where they raise and defend their young. These hiding places are usually holes in the ground where the young hide from enemies. They offer no protection from wind or rain. Guinea pigs don't construct elaborate burrows for their offspring the way most other rodents do. They don't have to, though, because their young are almost fully developed at birth. The guinea pigs leave their shelter to search for food. Their range is about 1 to 4 yards (1 to 4 m). This strategy has proved quite effective, because in many areas of South America guinea pigs have become a nuisance species.

up and down ramps and play on the different levels. Make sure that the cage and accessories are of good quality, though. Wire or plastic ramps are not suitable for our little rodents' sensitive feet. In guinea pig forums and home

An Aquarium or Terrarium as a Cage?

Fortunately, guinea pigs are seldom kept in aquariums or terrariums, although I have seen this on occasion. So here are a few words on the subject. The only positive thing about an aquarium or terrarium is that it allows the animal to have visual contact with its surroundings.

In an aquarium or terrarium, the air stagnates, and this poor ventilation is bad for your rodents. Many animals—including guinea pigs—give off toxic ammonia gas along with their urine. You are certainly familiar with the scent; the pungent odor in filthy cages is ammonia. The higher relative temperature and humidity in a space with enclosed sides increase the airborne urine ammonia levels. Airborne ammonia is highly absorbed in nasal passages and damages the cilia and skin present. This damage predisposes your pet to respiratory illness. In addition, aquariums and terrariums are very difficult to clean, and attaching hay racks and water bottles to them presents problems. Aquariums are for fish, not guinea pigs.

Cage Accessories

Our house doesn't really feel like a home until we've decorated it to suit our tastes. Admittedly, taste depends on the individual and the culture, but all people have the same basic needs. It's no different for guinea pigs.
Hide box: A hide box is important for guinea pigs. As herd animals, they seek close contact with others of their kind. That's why there must be enough room for all in the box. I even put a second smaller hut in the cage for my bunch, just in case one of the little critters isn't in the mood for company. My trio often changed company. On some days, all three slept together peacefully in the box; other days the male went off by himself and slept in the "one-room bungalow." Sometimes one of the females chose to be alone. Why they acted this way fascinated me. Unfortunately, weeks of study yielded no clues. Neither quarrels nor pregnancy seemed to trigger this behavior. Be that as it may, I recommend wooden rather than plastic hide boxes, although plastic is easier to clean. Wood is especially important for tooth care, even though a wooden house obviously cannot withstand the incisors for long. A house damaged by gnawing must be replaced. **Tip:** If a guinea pig chews off and swallows bits of plastic, this can cause health problems.

New houses are immediately tested for coziness.

Food bowls: Choose untippable food bowls made of porcelain or clay so the food won't land in the bedding. As a rule, two food bowls are usually enough—one for pellet mixes, the other for greens and fresh foods (see Nutrition, beginning p. 64).

Sipper bottle: The water bottle is made of glass or plastic; hung on the cage wire, it takes up very little room in the cage, and the water stays clean. Don't worry—even youngsters quickly learn how to use a sipper bottle. A little trick speeds up the learning process: Moisten the tip of the sipper tube, so that the youngster licks it and inadvertently opens the ball-point valve. In no time he'll figure out what he has to do to get the water.

Hay rack: The daily hay ration belongs in the hay rack and not on the floor of the cage. A plastic hay rack closed on all sides and open only on the top is a practical choice. It can be hung from the wires on the outside of the cage. This way the guinea pigs can pull stalks of hay out of the rack from inside the cage. Hay racks like this take up no

space in the cage and the hay doesn't land on your floor.

Bedding: A variety of bedding materials are available for your guinea pig. A layer of commercial wood shavings about 4 to 6 inches (10 to 15 cm) thick is effective. These shavings are commonly softwoods. Cedar shavings are not recommended, as cedar releases toxic aromatic hydrocarbons. Hay, straw, and paper bedding are all very good alternatives.

Decorating with style

You can easily improve the cage décor with a little ingenuity and imagination.

Partitions: Movable partitions, preferably those made of wood, are a great way to make your guinea pigs' dream home more interesting. You can change the layout of the cage simply by rearranging the walls. That stimulates curiosity and encourages activity of the occupants. Furthermore, subordinate animals can even hide behind a partition to avoid the herd boss, if necessary.

The color green: You have to chuckle at some of the preferences of our little

◄ *Huts made of woven grass are fun to chew and make great toys. And when your piggy is tuckered out afterward, he can even take a little nap inside. How practical!*

rodents. Professor A. Bilsing and her team discovered that guinea pigs have a weakness for green. Other colors will do, but green is their favorite. Light-colored floor coverings, like white tiles, caused stress, whereas the little rodents were visibly happier on a dark surface. That makes sense, because in the wild the guinea pigs leap and run around on green grass or brown earth. Heredity asserts itself, even in our domesticated animals.

Beyond the Cage: The Exercise Area

Although we don't know a great deal about the life of guinea pigs' wild fore-bearers, this much is certain: They had to keep moving in order to survive. Finding food and evading hungry predators day after day is not for the indolent.

Our cuddly pets need exercise, too. It's rooted in their genes. No matter how large the cage, it can't satisfy their need for exercise. That's why I urge you to give them an exercise area indoors or, better yet, outside in the yard or on the balcony (see beginning on page 42). Two hours of out-of-cage time per day are the minimum (see Hazards, p. 103).

An indoor exercise area

If you can't give your guinea pigs an entire room for their exercise area and want to keep them safely corralled, then I recommend attaching a prefab playpen to the cage. This way you can leave the little critters alone in the room—without supervision—and not worry about it. The pet supply store carries collapsible enclosures that are easy to assemble as well as pens made of

CHECKLIST

A Recipe for Contentment

Would you like your guinea pig to be truly happy? Here are a few important requirements.

- ○ Two nest boxes are better than one. One of the two should be large enough for all to snuggle in.

- ○ Subdivide the cage with partitions. That gives the subordinate animals an opportunity to hide (see page 38).

- ○ It's not the number of toys that's important; remember instead that "variety is the spice of life."

- ○ Chewable items for wearing down the teeth are a must (see page 75).

individual fence panels (see photo, page 40). Pens like this come in a wide variety of sizes. As always, though, the bigger, the better. To make it easier for the guinea pigs to climb out of the cage to "freedom," place a brick in front of the opened cage door. Then lay a small flexible wooden bridge across the opening so that the guinea pigs can go in and out of the cage comfortably (see photo, page 34). The animals can freely choose to go exploring or stay home. If one member of the group is eager for action, then the others usually follow quickly. After all, curiosity is catching.

▲

An enclosure placed around the cage allows ample freedom of movement.

Protect your floor: Now you're faced with a little problem. What can you put beneath the playpen so that your floor doesn't get dirty? Guinea pigs don't like tiles; they're smooth and cold, and that can be unhealthy. On the other hand, you have to protect your floor from urine and feces. Training guinea pigs to use a cat-type litter box is difficult. I must confess, I have never succeeded in teaching my guinea pigs to do it. I don't believe it's possible, because the digestive system in herbivores functions quite differently from that in carnivores and omnivores. I have never seen a housebroken cow, to say nothing of a horse, but I have seen lions and tigers like this. Now here's my suggestion: Place a thick sheet of plastic on the floor (for example, a pond liner); over this put a layer of newspaper to absorb any urine that soaks through; then as

the top layer use a chewable mat made of rice straw, reeds, or maize (inexpensive items available at a home-improvement center). Durable carpet remnants (without loops) will also serve the purpose, although not quite as well.

Furnishing the exercise area: Suitable furnishings for the exercise area include cardboard tubes; shoe boxes with holes to run through; cork, sisal, or wood tunnels; boards and branches to chew on; and small hurdles to jump over. The setup can easily be changed, making it easy to provide the occupants with new and exciting challenges. You can find additional suggestions for "activities" in Chapter 6, beginning on page 96.

Tip: Never overload the cage and adjoining exercise area with too many objects. The animals must be able to travel short distances without immediately stumbling over something.

Basic Equipment
at a Glance

Furnishings

The cage furnishings affect your guinea pigs' sense of well-being. When buying accessories, make sure they are guinea-pig friendly. They have to please your pets, not you.

◀ Manger

A manger like this keeps greens out of the dirty bedding. The advantage of a movable manger is that it can be set up in the outdoor enclosure as well as in the cage.

◀ Hide box

A hide box with a flat roof is best. Your guinea pigs can climb up on it and enjoy the view or avoid another guinea pig. Most hide boxes have no floor, but that's not a problem.

ipper bottle ▶

ter a few tries, guinea pigs uickly learn to drink from e sipper bottle. Unlike a owl, a sipper bottle keeps e water clean and the bedng dry.

Food bowl ▲

Bowls made of stoneware are difficult to overturn and easy to clean. They are especially good for commercial pellet mixes. The animals enjoy eating together from the bowl.

Outdoor Enclosure and Balcony

For guinea pigs, time spent outdoors is just like a vacation in the mountains or at the beach for us. They get fresh air, a change of climate, exercise, and plenty of sensory stimulation. So treat your pets to some time in the great outdoors.

 Do you have a yard or a balcony? Then don't hesitate to provide a fresh air oasis for your pets. Exploring a stimulating environment makes the animals more confident and less fearful. As a result, your guinea pigs will be better able to bond with you. You'll see how happy your guinea pigs are when you come into the yard or onto the balcony and want to spend time with them.

Fresh Air Does Them Good!

The backyard is ideal because they are exposed to the fresh air and changing weather conditions there. That improves their immunity, protects against diseases, and prevents weight problems. Even guinea pigs need an obstacle course to strengthen their muscles and help them feel their best. Out-of-cage time doesn't just develop an animal's body, though; it's also good for the mind. Here in the outdoors they are constantly exposed to new stimuli and sensory impressions. That arouses their curiosity and prevents boredom. Animals allowed to live like this are mentally fit and active. Don't worry—the little rodents can easily cope with sun, rain, and breezes; they just can't tolerate extreme heat. No doubt about it, guinea pigs enjoy experiencing new things in

the outdoor enclosure, the yard, or the house. Be careful, though, because our little pets are sensitive to stress. A mixture of the familiar and the new works best. Guinea pigs need familiar reference points, such as their hide box or a partition with their "perfume."

Change of Climate

Although it's true that guinea pigs are adaptable and can get used to different temperatures, this requires a certain amount of training. An animal that lives primarily indoors must be acclimated gradually to the fresh air, colder ground, wind, and showers; otherwise the danger of catching cold is too great. The open-air season begins with the first warm days in spring and ends in fall when the weather turns damp and cold. Put the animals outdoors for the first time on a fine day when the temperature is above 54°F (12°C). At the beginning of the season, I leave the animals in the movable outdoor enclosure for just two to three hours (see page 43) and keep a close eye on them.

The outdoor enclosure is furnished sparsely at first: the familiar hide box from the cage and a large, roomy, weatherproof shelter where the whole group can retreat if danger threatens and where they can find protection

▲
Adventure in the backyard. Suddenly you're face to face with strange creatures like this snail.

from rain, heat, and wind (see The hutch, page 44). As soon as the guinea pigs start spending a lot of time in the shelter, I remove the indoor hide box. Once the guinea pigs have accepted their new home, I increase their time outdoors from two to three hours in the beginning up to five or six hours a day. Now I'm sure that the animals can handle the vagaries of the weather and know that their house offers them shelter. In the evening I bring my guinea pigs back indoors, first of all for safety, and secondly to spend time with them, cuddle them, and play with them.

The Movable Outdoor Enclosure

The advantage of a movable outdoor enclosure is obvious. The enclosure can be set up in different spots. This way the animals can always enjoy a new view and fresh lawn that has not been soaked by their own urine. Some stores carry collapsible outdoor pens or prefab enclosures made of wire panels where the guinea pigs can spend a few hours. I recommend these enclosures only if your yard is safe from dogs and cats and you can see the guinea pigs from the house. A net cover offers protection from birds of prey but won't withstand dogs and cats. Pet stores also sell sturdy outdoor enclosures made of heavy-duty wire. Wire walls, a wire roof, and a shelter (house) are sold as a unit. The guinea pigs are safe in these enclosures. The only disadvantage is that these outdoor pens are usually not very big. The largest that I have seen was 6½ feet (2 m) long and 20 inches (50 cm) wide. This is enough room for two animals if they also get regular out-of-cage exercise. For small yards and for people who don't want to build an enclosure themselves, this is a good solution.

The outdoor enclosure must be **as large as possible** to provide an enriched environment for your pets.

Building an enclosure yourself
You can design and build an outdoor enclosure to suit your needs.
Size: Naturally, I cannot give precise guidelines, since it all depends on the size of your yard. In principle, the bigger the enclosure, the better. My little group of guinea pigs has an outdoor enclosure measuring 6½ feet × 5 feet (2 × 1.5 m).

From spring to fall, life is good in an outdoor enclosure.

Construction begins: To build the enclosure, you need wood lath and wire mesh. The openings in the mesh should be small enough to prevent your guinea pigs from squeezing through; they should also keep out raccoons, rats, and other small predators. The individual sections of the frame should be between 12 and 16 inches (30 and 40 cm) high. The wire mesh is stretched over a wooden frame. The individual wooden frames are joined using wing screws so that you can easily assemble and disassemble the pen. For a cover, I recommend another sturdy wooden frame with somewhat heavier tight-weave wire mesh. Attach two hinges to one side of the cover and one or two latches to the other so that you can easily open it like the lid of a chest.

The hutch: A carpenter built me a small "villa" as a weatherproof shelter for my guinea pigs, but with a little skill, you can do it yourself. For two or three animals, a base measuring 16 × 16 inches (40 × 40 cm) and a height of 12 inches (30 cm) are sufficient. The floor of the hutch is made of solid, heavy wood. To keep the guinea pig's home off the ground, 1-inch- (3-cm-) high "feet" are nailed to the underside of the floor at each of the four corners. This slight elevation has two advantages: It protects the hutch from weathering and keeps the animals off the cold ground. So that you can easily remove the hutch from the base, you can screw blocks of wood 2 inches (5 cm) high to the four corners of the top side of the base to serve as anchors. The hutch rests on these wooden blocks. The walls and the roof of the hutch are made of solid wood ¾ to 1¼ inch (2 to 3 cm) thick. The roof is sloped slightly so that water can run

WHAT EVERY OUTDOOR ENCLOSURE NEEDS

ESSENTIALS FOR OUTDOORS

Hutch:	Constructed of solid wood with room for all the animals; lined with commercial bedding.	Protection from too much sun, rain, wind, and cold.
Eating area:	Preferably raised so that the food doesn't get dirty.	Put dry and fresh foods on a stone slab.
Activities:	A hollow log or cork tubes to crawl through and climb over.	Don't put too many toys in the enclosure. There has to be enough room for the animals to run around.
Protection:	A sturdy cover made from a wooden frame and wire mesh.	In a permanent outdoor enclosure, provide additional protection for the floor (see page 47).

off. The doorway is about 4 inches (10 cm) wide and 4¾ inches (12 cm) high. The construction is relatively heavy to avoid heat loss and provide protection from potential predators (cats). To turn the house into a fortress, you can also place some heavy rocks on the roof. The outer walls and roof are painted with nontoxic, water-repellent paint. I put a ½-inch- (1-cm-) thick plank in front of the entrance to make it easier for the animals to get in and out, and I cover the floor of the hutch with a thick layer of commercial bedding. The detachable top makes it easy to clean the hutch when it gets dirty.

Furnishing the enclosure: Essentially, this is the same as the indoor playpen (see page 40). The eating area must be covered so that the food doesn't get wet. One way to do this is to lay a board on the roof above the eating area. I place the food bowl on a flat stone slab to keep the food from getting dirty. I also serve their greens on a stone slab. I hang the sipper bottle from the wire mesh. I've had good results with branches and hollow logs that they can crawl through and climb over. Don't overload the pen with toys. This is where the animals should interact with nature, and nature offers plenty of variety.

Location: A site half in sun and half in shade is best. If this isn't possible, create some artificial shade by placing a light-

In the Outdoor Enclosure

▶ **1** **This wooden toy** can be used for "gymnastics" and is also safe to chew. That's good for both body and teeth.

▶ **2** **This movable outdoor enclosure** made from individual wire panels is suitable only if you can keep an eye on the animals.

▶ **3** **A fresh-air oasis** on the balcony. When setting up the enclosure, make sure there is no chance your animals might fall.

weight board on one part of the cover or else stretch a tarp (canvas) over the top. Shade is important, because the little rodents are susceptible to heatstroke (see page 92). They can even play under the tarp or board when it's raining. If the spot is drafty and windy, I recommend that you fasten a sheet of plastic to the sides of the wooden frame with nails or, better yet, screws. Drafts contribute to illness in guinea pigs. An obvious precaution, but one easily overlooked, is to check the site for poisonous plants (see page 75).

Tip: When setting up the outdoor enclosure, make sure that the area is level so that the frame sits directly on the ground, leaving no gaps through which an animal could slip. To be safe, you can even anchor the wooden frame in the ground with stakes.

The Permanent Outdoor Enclosure

Keeping guinea pigs outdoors all year round is no easy matter and requires a lot of work. First of all, the problem of temperature must be solved. Guinea pigs prefer warm temperatures (see page 34). It has been reported that they can adapt to temperatures as low as 50°F (10°C).

I don't dispute that, but we don't know how the little rodents feel about it. If you seriously intend to keep the animals outdoors, you must make sure that they have a winter-proof hutch. A cat flap allows the animals to go outdoors whenever they like. This hutch must be cleaned frequently, because damp bedding and straw don't provide warmth. It would be ideal to have one

part of the enclosure and the hutch sheltered by the roof of the house so neither rain nor snow could get in. With a location like this, you can suspend a heat lamp to provide more pleasant temperatures. Heat lamps specially designed for animal housing are available in electrical supply stores. Construction of the permanent outdoor enclosure is similar to that of the movable one; it's just built to be sturdier. You have to prevent nocturnal break-ins by raccoons, foxes, and cats. One problem is the floor. You wouldn't believe how quickly food attracts other animals. That's why it's a good idea to cover the floor of the enclosure with slabs of rock or fine wire mesh and put a thick layer of soil over it.

Tip: Keeping your guinea pigs outdoors presupposes that your animals live in a herd so that they can keep each other warm. Purebred animals with long hair cannot be housed like this.

Life on the Balcony

An indoor pen can easily be set up on the balcony (see page 40). When doing this, take the following precautions: Block any openings the guinea pigs could squeeze through so there is no chance they could fall or injure themselves. Cover up hazardous spots like this with wire mesh or bricks that the animals cannot shove aside. Provide

TIP

No strangers allowed!

Never put strange guinea pigs, such as a neighbor's pets, in the enclosure with your animals. It will disrupt the existing hierarchy among your "piggies" and can lead to quarrels or fights. Even if everything looks peaceful, there is a "war" raging inside your animals, and levels of stress hormones rise.

MY PET

What do your guinea pigs prefer?

Try to discover in which outdoor enclosure your guinea pigs feel more content, active, and curious. Are there differences between individual animals? Does the "boss" lead the way when it comes to exploring?

The test begins:

Set up an enclosure with just a shelter and fence, but no furnishings. Place the animals inside for two hours a day, two days in a row. Write down what the animals do. How long, for instance, do they spend running around or sleeping? Do they make sounds? Where do they stay, and so on? On the third day, furnish the enclosure with toys, partitions, and tunnels. Does anything change?

My test results:

protection against rain and sun. To keep the critters as well as their food and house dry, stretch a transparent tarp overhead when it rains; cover just the house and eating area, though. A net placed over the enclosure offers protection against birds of prey. A stone floor is not good for the animals. Cover the floor with reed or maize mats. The furnishings are like those of the indoor exercise area and the outdoor enclosure (see pages 40 and 45).

Life in a Rabbit Hutch?

Not only is this sort of hutch far too small, but it is also much too cold in winter. Given the choice between different ambient temperatures, I have not observed any guinea pigs choosing a temperature below 50°F (10°C).

◀ *Exercise in the fresh air: The guinea pig really has to exert herself, and that keeps her healthy.*

Welcome
Home

Have you decided on at least two guinea pigs? What's important now is that the animals learn to trust you right from the start.

Selecting and Buying Your Guinea Pigs

When you see the cute youngsters sitting in the display cage at the pet store, you might be tempted to take two of them home with you right away. Be careful, though, because impulse purchases like this can lead to bitter disappointment. It's better to make careful preparations before you buy.

Guinea pigs are herd animals and bond with others of their kind as well as with humans. They suffer if they switch human partners too often. To make matters worse, their sadness is not as obvious as it is with dogs or cats. That's why I urge you to think carefully about whether you would like to keep guinea pigs.

Without a doubt, the little rodents are work, but then they give you and your children a lot in return. Unfortunately, it happens all too often that people get guinea pigs and then after a few weeks lose interest in the little creatures. The odyssey that usually follows is terrible for the animals. A pet can't just be exchanged like clothing.

Where to Find "Piggies"

There are many places where you can find the guinea pig of your choice:
- breeders
- pet stores
- friends
- animal shelters

Breeders

There are many good guinea pig breeders. You can find their addresses on the Internet. However, getting to know the breeder in person is a must. See for yourself whether the breeder is in business just for the money or because he or she loves animals. How can you tell the difference? Admittedly, it's not easy, but my years of experience with breeders of all kinds have taught me something surprising. A conversation reveals more than you might expect. If the breeder speaks disparagingly of the animals and treats them as mere objects, then stay away.

You will find that a breeder like this knows little about the animals. Housing

Once you're in your new home, the first thing to do is investigate everything carefully. ▶

conditions are usually not optimal, either. A good breeder knows exactly when the babies were born and can relate fascinating details about the parents and their offspring. That's how you know that the breeder is interested in the guinea pigs as individuals. Good breeders feel responsible for their animals, and that is reflected in the questions they ask you. They want to be sure their animals' new owners will be responsible, too. Naturally, a good breeder will also refuse to send guinea pigs through the mail.

Request references from a breeder. Prepare a list of questions for previous purchasers of this breeder's guinea pigs

and give the references a call. Also ask the breeder about any warranties they make regarding their stock. Some breeders will replace an ill or unsound pet. Very good breeders will take their livestock back if you need to give them up for any reason.

Pet stores

Don't decide to buy the animals the first time you visit the pet store. Why? Guinea pigs have a circadian rhythm. At certain times they are active, at other times they doze. In this respect, they're not much different from humans and other animals. If you want to see how curious and sociable these little rodents are, you have to catch them at the right moment. Ask the pet dealer where the animals came from. If they made a long journey, often confined in tiny transport cages along with many other unfamiliar guinea pigs, it's not unusual for them to be in a state of shock. This trauma takes a while to wear off, and the guinea pigs remain timid for a long time afterward.

Inspect the housing conditions in the pet store. The cages must be large and clean, and there should be a thick layer of small-animal bedding. It goes without saying that water and a hay rack must be available. Twigs, branches, or hard objects to gnaw are also important. There should always be several animals living in the cage—in this case, even dwarf rabbits make acceptable cage mates (see page 21). Several hide boxes should be available, depending on the number of guinea pigs. Young guinea pigs, in particular, are often very skittish and run into their hiding place right away at the least disturbance. This escape behavior is inborn in them.

CHECKLIST

Initial Health Check

- ○ The incisors are of equal length and growing normally.

- ○ The cheek teeth (premolars and molars) are not visibly misaligned.

- ○ The position of the feet is correct, and the toenails are straight.

- ○ The coat is glossy and dense with no bald spots.

- ○ The eyes are clear and not stuck shut.

- ○ The ears are clean and the nose is pink; there is no discharge.

- ○ The anal region is clean and not caked with feces.

Private owners

If your friends' or acquaintances' pets have offspring, this is a welcome opportunity to make your guinea pig dreams come true. In my opinion, this is ideal. You know the owners and their attitude toward their guinea pigs. You can easily check the animals' living conditions. You can take your time observing the animals before you make your selection. The guinea pigs benefit from this, too. They are changing owners only once. This avoids unnecessary stress.

Animal shelters

Naturally, every animal shelter is happy to find a good home for its charges. This is understandable, but not an easy task with guinea pigs. That's because guinea pigs are extremely social, but also very sensitive. The development of their personality depends heavily on their experiences when young as well as on their guinea pig companions. With shelter animals, you usually don't know their history. That involves a certain risk, which can be minimized only by careful observation. If the guinea pigs are tame and respond to little treats, then you can go ahead without worrying too much that you'll get a guinea pig with behavioral problems. It's best if the animal shelter can let you adopt an intact group of two or three animals.

Which Guinea Pig Shall It Be?

We humans have had a hand in the development of almost all domestic animals, breeding them to suit our tastes. This has not always worked to the advantage of our fellow creatures, because a supposedly beautiful appear-

When you buy your guinea pigs, make sure that the animals are lively and alert.

ance has its price. When the external features are changed, other hereditary traits are altered as well. Overbred animals are usually less robust and have a lower life expectancy. In guinea pigs, the extent of selective breeding is limited. Only 10 percent of our guinea pigs are purebred. The other 90 percent are domestic guinea pigs that adapted to life with humans centuries ago. Whether you decide on a purebred guinea pig or an ordinary domestic guinea pig is a matter of taste. I prefer the "normal" domestic guinea pig without excessively long hair. Smooth or normal hair is the type of coat that is closest to the original and requires the least care. Extremely long hair creates problems with hygiene, but what's even worse is that it hampers the guinea pig's movements. When buying a guinea pig, behavior and health matter most.

Proper Treatment

For her birthday, our seven-year-old daughter Maya is finally getting the two guinea pigs she has been longing for. What can we do so that, right from the start, Maya respects the unique personalities of her pets, handles them carefully, and so is protected from possible disappointment herself?

It says a lot for you that you are already concerned about the welfare of the animals as well as sparing your daughter any disappointment with her "dream pets." First of all, teach her as much as possible about the nature, needs, and proper treatment of these animals. Of course, this assumes that you know about these things yourself. "Package" your information in an interesting manner for your daughter. For instance, you could pick one or two characteristics of guinea pig life, like the fact that guinea pigs can hear very well (see page 14). You could show your child how stressful loud noises are for the animals by turning the volume on your stereo all the way up to high for a moment.

Proceed with care

Once you have brought the animals home, proceed as follows: You and your daughter should sit down together about 20 inches (50 cm) away from the cage and watch the goings-on of your four-legged friends. That's when you'll see each of these spirited creatures reveal its characteristics and personality. This is also a good opportunity to give the animals names. That way, they are no longer "nobodies," but rather unique individuals. Children want to stroke and cuddle their furry friends right away, and so they should, but they've got to know how and when.

Giving them time to acclimate

Before your daughter grabs a guinea pig and takes him out of the cage, the animal should first have learned to trust her (see page 59). He must come to the cage wires of his own accord when she calls his name softly and tempts him with a bit of food. That is essential for fostering the animal's trust. Otherwise, being grabbed and removed from the cage without warning triggers the animal's natural panic response. This is exactly how guinea pigs are seized by birds of prey, their greatest natural enemies. She can avoid scaring her pets this way by speaking to them, gently clasping an animal's neck with one hand, and sliding her other hand under his hind legs for support (see page 81).

Only after your child has mastered this "hold" can she take a guinea pig out of the cage or pen. Introduce her to the world of the guinea pig one step at a time.

A simple behavior test reveals much about the animals. Ask the caretaker at the pet store to reach into the cage as if to catch an animal. If the little critters scurry into a corner or into the hide box, that's good and normal. After all, guinea pigs are flight animals. Within a few minutes their curiosity should overcome their fright. They'll investigate to see what's going on. If one of the animals remains sitting apathetically in a corner, it could have health or behavior problems. At the pet store, it's difficult to determine if your future guinea pig is healthy and fit (see Checklist: Initial Health Check, page 52).

Age at Purchase

If you are a beginner pig owner, I recommend obtaining youngsters six to eight weeks old. They can be easily tamed. Try to buy two or three siblings at the same time. It seems expensive, but there are major advantages. The animals already know each other and get along well together. They will tolerate a change of environment more easily. This way feelings of abandonment and loneliness have little chance of developing. As a consequence, the guinea pigs are more curious and quicker to interact with you. It's great to provide older animals with a home, but without some "know-how," you shouldn't attempt this.

2 **To determine the sex,** press gently around the anus. In males, the penis protrudes clearly. Even beginners can easily determine the sex.

1 **In young female** guinea pigs, the genital region looks like the letter Y. The distance between the anal and genital openings is smaller in females than in males.

Acclimating Gently

Moving to new surroundings is stressful for all guinea pigs. That's why it's important to make the adjustment as easy as possible for them. Only then will the little critters learn to trust you and quickly become tame.

When guinea pigs are removed from their familiar surroundings, it's very stressful for them at first. That's why the trip to their new home should go as smoothly as possible.

Bringing Them Home

Drive straight home after buying your guinea pigs. Be sure the trip doesn't take too long, because the animals will be frightened. Put the guinea pigs in a plastic travel carrier for the trip. Many pet stores offer cardboard boxes for transporting animals, but a plastic travel carrier is better (see photo, page 82). The animals can move around freely in it and the air is much better. Although it's true that carriers like this aren't cheap, they can always be used again, for example, when you take your pets to the veterinarian or on a short trip. During the drive, don't put the carrier in the trunk of the car; place it on a seat instead and secure it with a seat belt if possible. When you're bringing your pets home, a handful of old bedding in the carrier will provide them with the familiar smell of their old cage while giving them a feeling of security.

Once you arrive home, place the carrier in the cage and open it. But first remove all the cage furnishings except for the hide box, food bowl, and water bottle.

Scatter a handful of shredded carrot on the cage floor as an enticement and leave the rest to the new occupants. Sooner or later their curiosity will get the upper hand, and they'll begin to explore their new home. As soon as they start to eat and drink, they've successfully cleared the first hurdle in the acclimation process.

The Guinea Pigs in Their New Home

For the first few hours, the little critters just sit in the cage, peaceful and calm. Neither facial expression nor behavior gives a clue as to what's going on inside them. Dogs and cats, on the other hand, are an open book. You can understand what they're feeling right off the bat. But hidden behind the guinea pigs' cool façade is a sensitive little creature. Every change in living conditions and every unfamiliar situation can cause them stress. Moving into the strange world of a new owner is a drastic change for guinea pigs.

Tip: If you already have guinea pigs at home, quarantine newcomers for two to three weeks and always wash hands between handling pets.

These two guinea pigs have known each other since they were little. Don't worry; even a pair of animals will become tame.

That's why you should approach your new family members with patience and sensitivity. They'll show their appreciation for it by beginning to interact with you. In the very first days, you'll lay the foundation for a happy, lifelong friendship.

Things to Avoid in the Beginning

Make the acclimation period easier for the animals by avoiding the following:

▶ Slamming doors, shrill sounds, and hectic activity all frighten the guinea pigs.

▶ Surprising, but true: Absolute silence is as stressful for guinea pigs as shrill sounds.

▶ Sudden movements above the cage trigger innate anxiety in the guinea pigs. That's because what approaches from above could be a dangerous bird of prey. Eventually, this anxiety disappears.

▶ Don't allow dogs and other pets near the animals at the beginning of the acclimation phase.

▶ Frequently switching bright lights on and off can trigger panic reactions.

▶ As long as the animals are still timid and fearful, they should not be handled or held.

▶ Don't clean the cage until the occupants are used to you and their new environment.

▶ Don't move the food bowls.

▶ Don't pick up the hide box.

Building Trust

▶ **1** **Approach the guinea pig** carefully and speak to her softly. The cage door remains closed for the time being.

▶ **2** **"Tempt" the guinea pig** with treats like a piece of carrot.

▶ **3** **Once the animal** has overcome her fear, open the cage door so that nothing more stands between you and your guinea pig.

To Establish Trust

▶ Do not reach in and grab your guinea pig.
▶ Call your guinea pig to you using a soothing voice.
▶ Avoid loud noises.

Guidelines for Acclimating Without Difficulty

All animals, whether large or small, fat or skinny, are unique individuals. To what extent they can develop their personality differs from species to species and depends on the complexity of the brain. Each of my guinea pigs was different: Some were more courageous and curious, others more shy and cautious. A few learned very quickly, whereas others took a very long time to catch on. Guinea pigs are individuals with their own personalities and demands. Respect the individual traits and idiosyncrasies of the animals. That will make it easier for them to acclimate and learn to trust you.

The scent of their own cage reassures them and makes them feel at home. That's why you should clean only the heavily soiled areas of the cage in the first weeks. Solitary guinea pigs need a great deal of attention. They panic much more easily than animals that live in a herd. Stress in these animals takes a long time to disappear. If another guinea pig is nearby, their agitation subsides much faster.

The social behavior of guinea pigs differs markedly from that of other herd animals. Apes pick lice off each other, horses and cattle lick each other, and parakeets groom each other with their beaks. Guinea pigs, on the other hand, don't snuggle together or engage in social grooming. That leads to the mistaken assumption that others of their kind are not so important.

However, exactly the opposite is true. A partner is enormously important for your pet's well-being.

Never pick up a timid animal! Offer him carrots through the cage wires.

This piques his curiosity and encourages him. At the same time, he learns to recognize your scent.

Tip: If you are starting out with just one guinea pig—although I definitely don't recommend this (see page 20)—you should use a little trick to make it easier for the newcomer to acclimate: Place some of his old bedding in the cage and play a recording of sounds made by his former herd. Softly, though. Sound levels above 80 dB (a normal speaking voice is 65–70 dB) will frighten the animal. Smells and sounds calm the guinea pig and give him a feeling of security. Once the little fellow has made friends with you, you should give him a guinea pig companion. Share the friendship; that's good for everyone.

How Do Guinea Pigs Become Tame?

To hand-tame your guinea pig, you need to proceed with empathy and understanding. Avoid quick, frightening movements and always approach your animal from the front (see photos, above). The advantage is obvious: This way he can recognize you immediately by sight as well as smell. The familiar is less frightening. The first step in taming is to make the animal curious about you. He should approach you on his own, voluntarily and without force. That's a fundamental principle and

TIP

Hand-raised animals

Be careful with guinea pigs that were hand-raised and are fully imprinted upon humans! These animals often have difficulty fitting in with an existing group and are dependent on our care.

MY PET

"Daredevil" or "scaredy-cat"?

You can find out what type of personality your guinea pig has in the very first hours. Brave or timid animals behave differently in their new environment, especially if other cage mates are present.

The test begins:

Write down all the types of behavior that your guinea pigs display. Does one of them immediately retreat into the hide box? Then this one has a rather timid and fearful disposition. Does the guinea pig frequently turn to one or more of the cage mates? Plucky animals seek contact with members of their herd or a cage mate. Shy animals usually start by getting acquainted with their surroundings and sniffing at the cage furnishings.

My test results:

applies to all animals, be they lions, tigers, or parakeets.

Taming, Step One

Arouse his curiosity. But how can you make a guinea pig curious about you?

Approach the animal with the cage door closed. Position yourself at eye level with him near the cage. Remain there quietly for a few minutes. And now here's the trick: Imitate the guinea pig's sounds. No guinea pig can resist its own sounds. In case you find it difficult to imitate him, use a small cassette recorder with a tape of guinea pig voices.

Taming, Step Two

Win his trust. With guinea pigs, the way to the heart is through the stomach.

Rub your hands with bedding from his cage. Now you smell like guinea pig, too. Then open the cage door and show the animal something like a fresh dandelion leaf. As you're doing this, call his name softly. A long-drawn-out "good" also has a calming effect on the guinea pig.

Taming, Step Three

Reinforce his trust. From the guinea pig's point of view, you are a sort of "lucky charm." Thus far, the animal has had only good experiences with you and so has come to associate you with everything positive. This trust can be further developed.

Tempt the guinea pig out of his cage with some greens. So that the road to freedom doesn't seem so difficult for the little fellow, build him a bridge by laying a board on the plastic tray of the cage. The pet store also sells flexible wooden ramps that make it much easier for him to climb in and out of the cage. Practice makes perfect, so repeat these exercises several times.

Taming, Step Four

No more fear. Now the ice is broken. The guinea pig decides on his own that he wants to interact with you and even lets you scratch him gently under the chin. You've scored your first point. Your second comes when you stroke his back with your finger. If the guinea pig no longer shies away, then he is hand-tame. Nothing more prevents him from exploring his surroundings. Now you'll see just how inquisitive the little rodents can be. Of course, you have to provide a way for him to return to the cage safely and without fear, because that is the place where he feels most secure. Now you'll get to know a completely different side of your guinea pig. The frightened little creature that was so easily stressed has developed into an individual who tackles new challenges with confidence and tries to master them.

When the Guinea Pig's Partner Dies

A solitary guinea pig is no guinea pig at all. So please, buy your piggy a new partner, preferably one that's the same sex as the deceased friend. Give the two some time to get used to each other. Not every little quarrel is dangerous; instead, they resolve the question of who's boss. It has been my experience that a younger newcomer will adapt more easily than an older one.

Once the guinea pig is tame, she will enjoy daily attention from her owner.

▼

Questions on Husbandry and Acclimation

? I would like to get my two-year-old dog Susie used to my two guinea pigs. Is that possible?

If your dog has no pronounced hunting instinct, this should be possible. My dogs have had no trouble learning to live with guinea pigs. This assumes that you proceed carefully. How do you go about getting the animals used to each other? Make the dog lie down in front of the guinea pig cage. Speak softly to her and praise her. With a carrot, tempt the guinea pigs to come close to the side of the cage. Meanwhile, give your dog a treat. The dog must keep very still so that the guinea pigs aren't startled. This way, each will learn to recognize the scent of the other and accept the other's presence as perfectly normal. Repeat this exercise five to ten times. If the guinea pigs and the dog show little interest in each other, then hold the guinea pig in your lap with the dog beside you.

Pet both animals at the same time. Eventually, the dog will learn that guinea pigs are not prey and the guinea pigs will learn that the dog is peaceful.

? I've heard that guinea pigs become tame faster if there is no hide box in the cage. Is that true?

Regardless of whether it is true or not, you should never use this sort of coercive method with these animals. In the wild, guinea pigs live in shelters where they take refuge when danger threatens. This is part of their innate behavioral repertoire. If there is no hiding place, serious behavioral problems will result. For this reason, you absolutely must provide a hide box.

? Is it possible to keep just one guinea pig?

The answer is an unequivocal no. Guinea pigs are definitely herd animals. A

human cannot take the place of another guinea pig because the animal doesn't bond strongly with a person the way dogs and other animals do. Although well-chosen rabbits, cats, and dogs can provide companionship, guinea pigs really do need other guinea pigs for their well-being.

? Can I keep my guinea pigs in my large, roofed aviary (12 feet × 6 feet [4 × 2 m]) during the summer?

Parakeets and cockatiels are probably not disturbed by guinea pigs. They may even regard guinea pigs as a welcome diversion. Guinea pigs are not afraid of the birds, either. Nothing in the behavior of the two animals argues against it.

Hygiene, though, does present a problem. The guinea pigs come in contact with bird droppings, and the birds are exposed to guinea pig feces. Fecal matter often carries disease, so in my opinion it would be

too risky to house birds and guinea pigs together in the same cage.

? **Are there differences in the behavior of various guinea pig breeds?**

As far as I know, there have been no scientific studies on this question. Some guinea pig owners believe that long-haired animals are more lethargic and easier to keep, but these are just individual opinions. On the other hand, there is a definite difference in behavior between wild cavies and domestic guinea pigs. See the chart on page 10 for elaboration of the difference between wild cavies and domestic guinea pigs.

? **Is it possible to take guinea pigs for a walk like, for instance, rats?**

I once observed this in England. A young woman was taking a leisurely stroll through the park with her guinea pig in her arms. Several times I saw people taking their pets for a walk in a travel carrier. I don't think that the guinea pigs enjoyed it very much. Unlike rats, they are much more sensitive and timid. I would advise against it.

? **A salesman at the pet store recommended that I buy one guinea pig to start and then get a second one later on. He claimed this would make the animals become tame faster.**

Exactly the opposite is true. For guinea pigs, being alone is a shock. That's why you should start by getting at least two animals at the same time. The guinea pigs support each other, and each relieves the other's

anxiety. They tolerate the transition from the pet store to your home more easily.

? **When I grab my guinea pig by the scruff of her neck, she screams pitifully, even though she has known me for a long time. What is the reason for this?**

When you grab your little friend like this, she immediately believes that she has been seized by a bird of prey. She inherited this fear of airborne dangers from her wild ancestors and reacts instinctively. It works better if she feels secure: Tempt the guinea pig to come over to you, speak to her softly, and then pick her up carefully (see page 59, 81).

Providing a Nutritious Delicious Diet

Guinea pigs are always eating; they must for proper digestion. But a lot depends on what they eat. A varied diet is important, as is their "daily bread," hay.

What You Should Know About Nutrition

The right combination of foods is important when feeding your guinea pigs. The guinea pig's body needs protein, carbohydrates, fats, minerals, and vitamins to keep functioning properly.

Guinea Pigs Are Herbivores

Over the millennia, an organism adapts to its environment, particularly its food supply. This ensures that a wide range of organisms can use all available food resources. There are specialists like the great panda, which eats only bamboo, omnivores like humans and pigs, and herbivores like the guinea pig. This adaptation to different types of food was accompanied by adaptations of the internal organs. The intestinal tract of a meat-eating carnivore is much shorter than that of a plant-eating herbivore. The guinea pig intestine is almost 8 feet (2.5 m) long. Mere numbers tell little, but a comparison illustrates just how enormous this is. In humans, the intestine is about 20 feet (6 m) long, and the average person is approximately 5½ feet (1.70 m) tall. Guinea pigs, however, are only 12 inches (30 cm) long. The little rodent's stomach is also comparatively huge. It holds ⅔ to 1 ounce (20 to 30 ml), about as much as a whiskey glass. That might not seem like much at first glance, but it is indeed when you consider that a guinea pig weighs about 28 ounces (800 g). A human weighing approximately 150 pounds (70 kg) has a stomach volume of about 7 ounces (200 ml). The list of adaptations goes on and on, but we're getting sidetracked here.

As you can see, we're closer to answering our question of what constitutes healthy food. The answer lies in the past, with the animal's ancestors. You just have to look at what they ate or are eating, and then you'll have a good idea of which foods are good for our domestic guinea pigs. Their ancestors' diet serves as a guideline for today's menu.

Every stalk a delight: Guinea pigs need fresh, high-quality hay every day.

65

Their ancestors' diet: What do wild cavies eat? Where these little creatures live, the food supply is not rich and varied, nor is their diet. They dine primarily on grasses and plants that contain a lot of crude fiber. These are by no means high-calorie foods. To get the energy they need, they must forage constantly. They are always eating, but the portions are small. A different strategy slow down because the muscles of the stomach and intestines are weakly developed. What this also means is that guinea pigs must not go without food.

Hay Is Especially Important

Hay is the "daily bread" of our little rodents. There must always be plenty of it available. Alfalfa or grass hay, such as timothy, may be fed. Hay should be clean, sweet smelling, and free of mold and dust. Hay provides the animals

DID YOU KNOW THAT . . .

. . . guinea pigs need to eat their feces?

Have you noticed that guinea pigs eat their own droppings? There's no reason to be disgusted. They don't eat normal droppings, but rather the soft, moist, grapelike feces called cecotropes. Digestion occurs primarily in the cecum, so cecotropes are very high in amino acids, vitamins, and fatty acids. Eating these droppings is a convenient way for guinea pigs to obtain all necessary nutrients.

is used by animals such as lions. They eat 40 pounds (20 kg) of meat at a time and then lie around doing nothing for several days. Both strategies are rooted in the genes of the two species, and each is successful in its own way.

Small portions: Offering guinea pigs large portions is wrong and unhealthy. Feed your guinea pigs small portions several times a day. Continually eating high-fiber foods is also important for medical reasons. It maintains intestinal motility (peristalsis). Without a constant supply of food, peristalsis would with the crude fiber necessary to keep their intestines functioning properly. As an additional benefit, constantly chewing on hay helps keep the growth of the incisors in check. Good hay consisting of different kinds of grass is the best basic diet. Guinea pigs enjoy eating clover hay and alfalfa hay as well as legume (bean and pea) straw. I usually buy meadow hay so I can offer my animals a wide variety of plants. It's best if the hay contains plenty of wildflowers along with the grass because they pro-

Guinea pigs are entirely herbivorous.
Good hay is essential for a healthy diet
and proper digestion.

vide important minerals. When you buy hay, make sure that these ingredients are listed on the package label. Also check to see that the hay is not too old.

How do you recognize fresh hay?

Old hay is very dusty and has a musty odor. It isn't sweet smelling. Hay shouldn't contain dirt, excrement, mold, or poisonous plants. If much of the hay has already broken into tiny pieces, it's better not to buy it. I've been satisfied with hay from the pet store, which is why I recommend that you go there first to buy hay. They carry different types of hay containing a wide variety of herbs. You can even buy individual dried herbs and mix them in with the hay.

Tip: Of course, no one is stopping you from collecting plants yourself. Be careful, though! Don't collect along heavily traveled roads. The toxic exhaust from cars contaminates the plants and can harm your guinea pigs as well. The same is true of plants from over-fertilized fields. Make sure that you don't collect any poisonous plants (see Addresses and Literature, page 141).

Nutritional Building Blocks

No doubt about it, hay is very important for guinea pigs. However, hay alone does not provide them with all the energy they need. That seems contradictory, because their wild cavy cousins subsist on grasses. There is a difference, though, between fresh grass and dry grass. In dried grass, unlike fresh grasses, many nutrients have already broken down. Guinea pigs, like all animals, need adequate amounts of protein (see Tip, below), fats, and carbohydrates to meet their energy requirements. Of course, they also need vitamins and minerals.

Commercial pellet mixes contain many nutrients, but fresh foods are still a must.

Protein

Why does the body need protein? It is important for the repair and renewal of the body, and protein breakdown supplies the body with energy. An example makes this impressively clear. If you look at yourself in the mirror and then do it again one month later, almost all of your skin cells will have been replaced by new ones. Very few of your old cells will have survived. New cells are continually being formed throughout the body, and proteins are required for this. Proteins are an important component of cell membranes. Cells are constantly dying and being born. This is a general biological principle and, naturally, applies to guinea pigs as well. A shortage of protein leads to deficiency diseases or death. Why does protein deficiency have such serious consequences? Quite simply, it's because muscles are composed primarily of protein. That's why bodybuilders and weightlifters have a high-protein diet. Your pets' muscles are also "protein packets."

The right amount of protein: How much protein does a guinea pig need to maintain its body? Scientists recommend 14 to 18 percent crude protein in the total daily feed ration. The following seeds and plants contain vegetable protein:

▸ Sunflower seeds
▸ Flaxseed, but be careful! Flaxseeds are very high in fat. Your guinea pigs can get chubby if they eat too many.
▸ Legumes such as soybeans and peanuts
▸ Grains
▸ Meadow hay and other greens

Carbohydrates

Starch and sugar are among the most familiar carbohydrates. They are found in foods like bread, pasta, and sweets. However, the biggest reservoir of carbohydrates is unavailable to humans and many animals. It is cellulose. Plants use cellulose to build their cell walls. Only herbivores like our guinea pigs can use this natural bounty because they can, with the aid of microorganisms and bacteria, break cellulose down to sugar. To be more precise, they do it with the aid of microorganisms and bacteria.

The herbivore's intestine is swarming with them, and were it not for these microscopic creatures, our guinea pigs would starve. Cellulose is found in all plants, including, of course, hay. Guinea pigs need carbohydrates for energy as well as for building and maintaining their body.

Fats

Proteins, carbohydrates, and fats are the foundation of a healthy diet. This trio supplies the energy. Nothing functions without them. However, the required amount of each one differs from species

TIP

Vegetable protein only

In contrast to animals like hamsters, guinea pigs are pure vegetarians. They can digest only vegetable protein. You wouldn't be doing your guinea pig a favor, then, if you decided to "spoil" him with something like cottage cheese or meatballs.

A carrot is loaded with vitamin A. The carotene in it is good for vision.

to species. Polar bears and seals, for example, need a lot of fat; guinea pigs, on the other hand, need more carbohydrates. In spring and summer, your guinea pigs can get the fat they need from green plants. In winter, you can supplement their diet with legumes and sunflower seeds.

Tip: Fat provides twice as many calories as an equal amount of carbohydrate or protein. Guinea pigs have a tendency to put on too much weight, so feed them only small amounts of high-fat foods.

Minerals

Minerals are salts of various metals. The body assimilates these salts, whereas most pure metals are toxic. All living things need minerals, and they perform a variety of functions.

A balanced mineral intake is important for guinea pigs. This mineral intake depends on the type of food and how it is given. For example, guinea pigs shouldn't eat too much calcium because it can lead to digestive problems. That's why you should feed only small amounts of alfalfa, broccoli, kohlrabi leaves, and parsley, all of which are high in calcium. On the other hand, your guinea pigs will get enough sodium salts if you follow the feeding recommendations in this guide.

Tip: If guinea pigs have a balanced and varied diet, they don't need salt licks.

Vitamins

Most creatures can make their own vitamin C. Only humans, apes, and guinea pigs are unable to do this. They

In the winter when the grass stops growing, you can plant some yourself in a flowerpot!

ter teaspoon of it over washed greens while they're still damp. It's best if you divide the amount into two doses a day, or an eighth of a teaspoon per feeding. These plants are high in vitamin C: nettles, parsley, peppers, broccoli, fennel, kiwi, kohlrabi, strawberries, white cabbage, clover, spinach, dandelion, corn, chicory, endive, cantaloupe, raspberry, guava, and orange. Carrots contain lots of vitamin A. I give multivitamins, which are sold in pet supply stores, when I have the impression that the animals are a bit under the weather. Otherwise, I am cautious about using them. The reason is quite simple: Multivitamins contain vitamin D, which can be harmful in excessive amounts. Too much of a good thing can lead to bladder stones.

have to get it through their diet. A vitamin C deficiency leads to serious diseases. A surplus of it is not harmful, because it is excreted in the urine.

Adult guinea pigs should get 10 milligrams per day, and pregnant females need 20 milligrams per day. These amounts are scientifically accurate, but who can weigh out quantities so precisely? As a rule, guinea pigs can satisfy their requirement for vitamin C with a balanced, varied diet of fresh foods like vegetables, fruit, and lettuce. However, vitamin C is not heat-stable and breaks down in plants that have been stored for a long time or exposed to heat and sun. To be on the safe side, I recommend that you add a pinch of vitamin C powder (from the drugstore or pharmacy) to your guinea pigs' food. This advice is especially true in winter when fresh foods are scarce. I sprinkle a quar-

Tasty Fresh Foods
at a Glance

◀ Greens

All guinea pigs love fresh wild plants like dandelions and plantain. Many other plants are also suitable for a healthy guinea pig diet (see Greens and Fresh Foods, page 73).

Vegetables ▶

Fresh, crisp vegetables like carrots, cucumbers, broccoli, or kohlrabi contain lots of vitamins and minerals. They are a must for your guinea pig's healthy diet.

◀ Fruit

Although fruit is a good source of vitamin C, many guinea pigs turn their nose up at it. In this case, satisfy your animals' vitamin C requirement with greens like dandelions or parsley.

71

Tip: As with humans, vitamin C helps protect guinea pigs against infectious diseases and colds. When my guinea pigs "sniffle and sneeze," I give them a double dose of vitamin C. Thus far I have had good results with this tip, which I got from a veterinarian. The animals are healthy again in no time. Do not take this as a recommendation to always self-treat your pig's illnesses. Any significant illness should be evaluated by a veterinarian.

FEEDING SCHEDULE FOR YOUR GUINEA PIG

TYPE AND AMOUNT OF FOOD

Daily

Hay must always be available.
Give one to two tablespoons of pelleted feed per animal per day. Distribute the portions over the day.

A handful of grass, some dandelion greens, a carrot, and a piece of cucumber. Fruit and vegetables in season. Apples, pears, broccoli, spinach (see page 74).

Fresh water must always be available.

Weekly

Once a week, give your guinea pigs hard bread and twigs to wear down their teeth.

It's impossible to be more precise about how much to feed, since daily requirements depend on the size of the guinea pigs and their level of activity.

Dry Foods and Fresh Foods

Guinea pigs are not at all demanding when it comes to food. However, when the same thing is on the menu day after day, they can become malnourished. Make sure they get a varied diet and foods to gnaw.

Commercial guinea pig diets are far better than their reputation. When used correctly, you can feed them to your guinea pigs without hesitation. Not only do they save time, but they're also easier.

What You Should Know About Commercial Diets

Commercial pellet mixes contain compressed hay, grains, oils, vitamins, and minerals. Pay close attention to the ingredients. Too much of a good thing is unhealthy; potential ingredients such as peanuts and sunflower seeds are loaded with calories. Also be aware that any added vitamin C will degrade so you must provide additional supplementation for your guinea pig.

How much to feed: Don't give more than one to two tablespoons of pellet mix per animal per day (see Feeding Schedule, page 72).

Mix your own food: Of course, you can also make your own mixture, but it takes a lot of experience to find the right combination of ingredients. I would advise against it for novice guinea pig owners. I have had good results with brand-name products and even avoid buying loose mixtures, because I have no guarantee they're fresh. When you're buying food, pay attention to the expiration date and the list of ingredients. Every brand has a somewhat different combination of ingredients, so I change brands after two or three purchases to get a greater variety of nutrients. Admittedly, that's not always the cheapest solution, but it ensures a varied diet. Here's another tip: Don't buy too much at one time, and don't store it for too long, because guinea pig food spoils easily.

Tip: Commercial pellet mixes are not complete diets. Your pets also need hay and fresh greens every day.

Greens and Fresh Foods

All greens aren't created equal. The nutrient content is greater in young plants than in older ones. In old plants, the amount of cellulose increases, and

TIP

What to do if your piggy is plump

Guinea pigs must not go without food (see page 66). If your guinea pig is overweight, you should simply be conscientious about omitting extra snacks like chew sticks or other fattening treats. A little fitness program might be appropriate now, too (see page 103 and following).

the plants become woody. The more your guinea pigs enjoy fresh grass in spring, the more careful you have to be. Spring grass contains a lot of protein and very little crude fiber. This can lead to digestive problems. At the beginning of the season, then, get your guinea pigs used to this juicy treat carefully. For example, put only half of the movable outdoor enclosure over a fresh patch of lawn. Guinea pigs need greens. They contain oils, vitamins, and trace elements. Depending on the season, my bunch gets wild plants, fruit, vegetables, and lettuce.

Wild plants: Dandelions are high in protein and calcium; because of the calcium content, though, don't give your pets too much. Nettles are rich in vitamin C and protein; however, the animals eat only dried and wilted plants. They are very nutritious. Goutweed is a weed, but guinea pigs love it. They also like cow-parsley. Guinea pigs have a tremendous appetite for other wild plants. For their own good, limit them and feed only small portions. The little rodents enjoy nasturtiums, field mint, coltsfoot, plantain, calendula, mugwort, chickweed, and chamomile. Some of my guinea pigs are particularly fond of one plant or another. Naturally, that doesn't encourage a balanced diet. Here's a tip: Don't feed them these plants every day; instead offer a variety throughout the week in small amounts.

Fruit: Despite what you might expect, not all guinea pigs enjoy fruit—mine don't. However, if your guinea pigs enjoy fruit, the fruit should be offered in small quantities throughout the week. Oranges, apples, pears, melon, kiwi, papaya, and strawberries are all good choices.

Vegetables: Don't feed vegetable scraps; instead, give them only fresh vegetables that you have washed under lukewarm water. Guinea pigs have varying degrees of preference for broccoli, cauliflower leaves, cucumbers, carrots, kohlrabi, celery, and zucchini.

Lettuce: You must also wash lettuce carefully. The little rodents are especially fond of endive; unfortunately, it contains substances that cause gas, so you can feed it only in small amounts. They also like head lettuce.

Tip: All cabbage family plants should be fed only in small amounts, because they cause flatulence.

The right way to feed fresh foods

You don't have to serve food to your animals on a silver platter, but it is a good idea to put it on a wooden board

◀ *This youngster eats dry food just like the adult. However, fresh foods and minerals are crucial for healthy development.*

or a small stone slab. This way the damp foods aren't soiled by the bedding, and the animals can really enjoy their crisp vegetables, fruits, and lettuce.

Caution, Poisonous!

At this point, I would like to point out some plants that are poisonous to guinea pigs. This is not a complete list of poisonous plants. Should you question a plant to which your pig has access, please call the veterinary poison control center.

Garden plants: pheasant's-eye, acacia, columbine, azalea, mercury, ivy, yew,

occasionally with chew biscuits and chew sticks made for guinea pigs from the pet store. Many guinea pigs are absolutely crazy about them. Don't give them too much, though—these chew treats are loaded with calories.

How Much Food Does a Guinea Pig Need?

It's difficult to say exactly, because how much you should feed depends on the caloric value and crude fiber content of the food. As a guideline, though, give the animals the equivalent of 4 percent of their body weight in ounces (grams)

Guinea pigs must have **chewable materials** like fresh twigs at all times. This is the only way they can wear down their continuously growing teeth.

monkshood, angel's trumpet, wisteria, laburnum, buttercups, autumn crocus, vinca, cherry laurel, crocus, lilies, nightshades, Solomon's seal, jimsonweed, juniper, and spurges.

Houseplants: cyclamen, Benjamin fig, crown of thorns, dieffenbachia, ferns, hoya, Jerusalem cherry, croton, oleander, poinsettia, and calla lily.

Chewables

Rodents' teeth grow throughout their life. Overgrown teeth prevent them from eating and cause injuries. Hard foods regulate the growth of their teeth. Suitable foods for chewing include hard bread as well as unsprayed twigs and branches from apple, pear, linden, and birch trees. Feel free to spoil your pets

every day. According to this, a guinea pig weighing 35 ounces (1,000 g) should get about 1½ ounces (40 g) of food a day. Guinea pigs should be given a variety of foods at a young age to have flexible eating patterns later on. Plentiful hay, some pellets, and a variety of fresh foods are needed every day.

Fresh Water

When it is very hot, guinea pigs take big gulps from their sipper bottle; usually, though, they drink very little. If they get lots of fresh juicy foods, they need about 3⅓ fluid ounces (100 ml) of water a day; otherwise it's 8½ to 33 fluid ounces (250 to 1,000 ml) daily. The water bottle must be filled and easily accessible at all times.

A tasty bit of carrot is concealed in the hay, but not for long.

The Correct Way to Feed Your Guinea Pigs

▶ Give the little critters their daily food ration in three small portions spread out over the day. If your job makes it impossible for you to follow this schedule, feel free to feed them in the morning and evening only.

▶ Hay must always be available in the rack. Don't put hay on the floor, or it will get dirty.

▶ In spring, introduce fresh greens slowly and carefully.

▶ Remove uneaten fresh foods from the cage. After the animals have stopped eating, I remove the leftovers. If there's a lot left, I put it in a plastic bag and refrigerate it.

▶ Pay attention to the ingredients in commercial guinea pig diets.

▶ Feed only small amounts of commercial diets (see page 73).

▶ The subordinate animals must also be able to get to the food without being disturbed. Guinea pigs usually eat peacefully together, but sometimes frictions can arise. Place a board in the cage so that the animals can't see each other.

▶ Make sure the animals get enough vitamin C every day (see page 70).

▶ Water must always be readily available.

MY PET

What tastes best to your guinea pig?

Scatter an assortment of foods around the outdoor enclosure or indoor play area during out-of-cage time. Now send your test subject on a hunt. This way you can find out which foods are your guinea pig's favorites and how well she can smell.

The test begins:

Hide bits of food so that the animal has to search for them. Then, after three or four initial attempts, observe several times in succession to see where the guinea pig runs first. The first few attempts could be accidents, because the guinea pig first has to learn where her favorite food is hidden. This test is first and foremost a test of smell. If you really want to discern your guinea pig's favorite foods, place small pieces of different foods spaced apart on a large plate and simply observe your pig at duplicate plates several days in a row.

My test results:

Grooming and Health Care

A clean cage and proper care are the basic requirements for keeping your guinea pig healthy. If an animal does get sick, though, you should take it to the veterinarian right away.

Proper Care Prevents Diseases

It's not hard to understand why hygiene is so important when keeping guinea pigs. Filthy cages and dirty animals attract disease like magic. That's why you have to keep everything clean, although you don't need to turn into a "clean freak."

A bird's plumage must be clean so that it can fly well. Many mammals groom themselves so that their coat will protect them from cold and be free of parasites. Grooming has an important function in the animal kingdom. It ensures the animals' survival. A creature that is infested with parasites usually gets sick, and its chance of survival sinks. Although animals don't take grooming to extremes the way we humans do, there must be a certain degree of cleanliness, especially with domestic animals.

Why Hygiene Is Important for Guinea Pigs

Regular cleaning of the cage and enclosure along with the furnishings is a basic requirement for keeping your guinea pigs healthy. Otherwise, bacteria, viruses, and fungi would have an easy time of it, and your cuddly pets would fall ill in no time. Grooming also plays an important role in health care. When guinea pigs are neglected, not only is their well-being affected, but they are also more susceptible to disease.

Cleaning the Cage and Furnishings

So that conditions in your guinea pigs' home never become unsanitary, you must clean it regularly.

Daily: Wash out all food and water containers with hot water and then dry them. It's best to clean the water bottle with a bottle brush and the metal sipper tube with a cotton swab. Then refill the food bowls and sipper bottles.

Weekly: Once a week I replace all the bedding in the cage. Incidentally, the commercial wood shavings that I recommend can simply be put in the trash

A glossy coat, clear eyes, and a clean nose—this animal is in perfect health.

or added to the compost pile. The bottom tray, cage wires, and cage furnishings can be scrubbed in the bathtub using hot water and a brush and then dried. Wash the partitions and bricks, too; the guinea pigs often mark them with urine (see page 15). The water should be really hot to kill off any germs but not hot enough to burn you. You can also use a dilute bleach solution (1 part bleach to 30 parts water) in warm water but must be careful not to splash the solution. When a bleach solution is used, the bowls should be thoroughly rinsed afterward. Sometimes bladder sludge collects in the bottom tray and is difficult to remove with a brush and water. Dilute citric acid (from the pharmacy) or softening in vinegar will help. Finally, rinse out the bottom tray thoroughly with clean water.

Tip: The pet supply store carries spray deodorizers. As their name says, they are supposed to reduce unpleasant odors and so let you postpone changing the bedding. Don't use them. Sprays like this just irritate your guinea pigs' delicate olfactory membranes while leading you to believe that the bedding is still clean. Nothing takes the place of regular cleaning.

Where to Put the Animals When You're Cleaning

While you're cleaning the cage, you should let the animals enjoy some free-roaming time in the room or in a pen. Maybe you even have an outdoor enclosure where the animals can stay during the cleanup. That way you avoid disturbing them and causing stress. My four guinea pigs have gotten used to these housecleaning episodes. I have the impression that they enjoy digging around in the fresh bedding. In any case, I notice a lot of activity in the cage after a major cleaning.

Tip: Naturally, guinea pigs that spend most of their time indoors shouldn't just be put in an outdoor enclosure when the weather is cold. If the change in temperature is too abrupt, your guinea pig can catch a nasty cold.

◄ *After you've completed the final chores, the animals can move back into their freshly cleaned cage. Many children enjoy setting up the cage again after it has been cleaned.*

Cleaning the Outdoor Enclosure

If your guinea pigs live year-round in a permanent outdoor enclosure, regular housekeeping is necessary here, too.
Daily: Clean the food bowls with hot water every day. The hutch must be lined with fresh hay or commercial small-animal bedding daily because guinea pigs soil their sleeping area with urine and feces.
Twice a week: "Muck out" the floor of the hutch completely and provide new bedding. If the box is very damp inside, you should first let it dry out thoroughly.
Weekly: Rake the ground inside the enclosure—depending on what it's covered with—and spread new litter, like bark mulch.

How to Pick Up and Carry a Guinea Pig

If you pick up your guinea pig clumsily, she will begin to squirm and can injure herself severely if she falls from even a low height. That's why it's important to pick up the animal gently and carry her securely. To pick her up, grasp her chest from below with one hand and support her hindquarters with the other (see photo, page 89.) To carry the guinea pig, place her on your bent lower arm, which should be held tightly against your upper body so that the animal cannot slip through. Use the other hand to keep her from falling down.

(see photo, page 89.)

CHECKLIST

Grooming and Housekeeping Schedule

Regular attention to hygiene is essential when keeping guinea pigs so that the animals stay healthy.

Daily:
- Wash out the water bottle and food bowls with hot water (don't use dish soap!).

- Check teeth, anus, eyes, nose, and ears.

- Brush long-haired breeds to prevent the coat from matting. Untangle mats in the hair with a comb or dematting tool.

- Short-haired guinea pigs groom themselves, but they love being massaged with the brush.

Weekly:
- Clean the cage and furnishings under hot water. Replace all the bedding. Clean the water bottle thoroughly, using a bottle brush.

Monthly:
- If bladder sludge has collected in the bottom tray, dissolve it using dilute citric acid or soften it with vinegar.

- Not absolutely necessary, but a good idea following an illness: disinfection with a mild disinfectant.

For your animals' health, it is important to
keep the cage clean and, if possible, examine
the animals carefully every day.

Grooming Guinea Pigs

Guinea pigs are relatively easy to care for. Nevertheless, it is important to watch the animals closely and examine them regularly. This is the only way you can spot signs of illness in time and, if necessary, have them treated by the veterinarian.

Toenails: Check the guinea pig's toenails weekly. If the nails get too long, this is often because the flooring is too soft. Overgrown toenails make it very painful for the guinea pig to walk. Make sure, then, that the animals can wear down their nails on a hard surface. Place one or more stone slabs in the cage or pen to provide different types of flooring. That helps keep the nails short. If they are still too long, don't

A travel carrier like this is ideal for taking your pet to the veterinarian.

hesitate to go to the veterinarian. He or she can show you how to trim them properly. Use special nail clippers (from the pet supply store) for this purpose. It's important to avoid injuring the blood vessels in the nail when you cut them. Hold the animal's foot against a bright light source, such as a table lamp. This way you can see exactly where the blood vessels are (the "quick"). Don't cut into the quick. If you should nick a vessel despite all your precautions, immediately apply pressure to the cut and cover it carefully with a spray bandage.

Teeth: You must inspect your guinea pigs' teeth regularly. Their incisors grow continuously, and if they are not worn down sufficiently by eating, they will grow inward. The sharp points of the teeth can cause the animal so much pain it will stop eating. Giving your guinea pigs hard food and twigs to chew (see Chewables, page 75) prevents dental problems. If the teeth do overgrow, have them trimmed by your veterinarian.

Eyes, ears, and nose: If the eyes, ears, or nose are soiled, they should be cleaned using a warm, damp cloth. One favorite home remedy, a solution of chamomile, is not suitable for guinea pigs. Chamomile causes hair loss in the animals. Warning! Constant and heavy discharges from the eyes, ears, and nose are often the first symptoms of disease. Don't hesitate to take a guinea pig like this to the veterinarian.

Anus: A dirty bottom usually indicates a serious illness. If the guinea pig has diarrhea, he may have been infected by intestinal parasites, be suffering from an infectious disease, or have dental problems. Improper diet or a vitamin C deficiency can also be at fault. Clean the soiled area with a warm, damp towel. Offer the guinea pig some good hay. Monitor his weight (see Weighing, page 86). If there is no definite improvement within two days or there are additional

symptoms, take your guinea pig to the veterinarian immediately. Diarrhea can quickly prove fatal for a small animal like a guinea pig.

Can a Guinea Pig Be Bathed?

Guinea pigs are somewhat afraid of water and catch cold easily (see bottom page 86). A bath, or better yet a shower, is appropriate only for an emergency like diarrhea or to get rid of parasites (see page 88).

To do this, place the animal under a gentle stream of lukewarm water until the coat is wet all over. The guinea pig will probably be immobilized by fear and allow you to proceed without resistance. On the other hand, he may put up quite a struggle. Make sure not to get water in his eyes, nose, or mouth. After the bath, dry the animal carefully

DID YOU KNOW THAT . . .

. . . guinea pigs shed their coats?

In spring and fall, guinea pigs usually shed their coat. They get their lighter summer coat in spring and the heavier winter coat in fall. You can see this clearly if your animals live in an outdoor enclosure from spring until fall. During this time it's quite normal for your guinea pigs to lose their hair. Guinea pigs that are kept exclusively indoors can lose hair all year long because of the constant room temperature. Pregnant females often lose hair at the end of their pregnancy and while they are nursing, especially in the belly and chest areas. Careful brushing with a soft natural-bristle brush helps to remove dead hair. Most guinea pigs enjoy being brushed because it feels like a wonderful, soothing massage.

with a warmed hand towel or even a hair dryer if he can tolerate the noise. Animals that live in an outdoor enclosure year-round should be put back outside only when their coat is completely dry and the pig has warmed up. Do not use heating pads because of the risk of burn injury. That can take several hours. Rain showers, on the other hand, are a pleasant treat for guinea pigs living outdoors. They remove dust and dirt from the coat and massage the skin. When the guinea pigs have had enough, they will head for shelter on their own. My bunch adores the rain.

Does the Coat Need Special Care?

American and Abyssinian guinea pigs really don't need our help caring for their coats. Only long-haired breeds are unable to keep their dense coat clean by themselves. Animals like this would have very little chance of surviving in the wild.

Coat care made easy: Long-haired guinea pigs must be combed and brushed several times a week. To do this, put the animal on a table or in your lap. Place a warmed hand towel beneath him—the guinea pig finds that pleasant. Run your hand over the animal's entire coat from the rump toward the head. In the process, feel for any abnormalities in the skin or matted areas in the coat. Use a soft brush and a wide-toothed comb for grooming. First comb the coat. Then brush it until it shines. The guinea pig's rear end gets dirty easily. Bits of hay and burrs get caught here if your guinea pigs live in an outdoor pen.

Removing mats and tangles: First separate the mat into small sections with your fingers. Then try to untangle it using a pintail comb or a knitting needle. If that doesn't work, you'll have to use a mat splitter (from the pet supply store). In summer, you should give your long-haired guinea pigs a haircut. This way you spare your animals the painful process of brushing out tangles; in addition, you'll prevent infections and infestations by parasites that like to settle in matted areas of the coat. Be sure to have a veterinarian take a look at extensive matted areas; you may need to have the animal sheared professionally.

How Do Guinea Pigs Groom Themselves?

If you watch your guinea pigs, you'll notice that they never groom each other. When it comes to personal hygiene, they are on their own; unlike mice and rats, guinea pigs get no help from other members of their group. Thus there is no mutual or—as it's referred to in scientific circles—social grooming.

Guinea pigs are clean animals and groom themselves constantly during the day. The dirtier they are, the more frequently they groom. Grooming follows a more or less fixed ritual. First the guinea pig lifts one or both front paws to her mouth, licks them, and then runs them quickly over her mouth, nose, the rest of her face, and her ears. Then she licks her sides and back, ending with the belly and genital area. If her tongue isn't enough to remove the dirt, she uses her teeth and nibbles at the soiled spot. She uses her hind feet to scratch the dirt from her head.

1 Weight: Adult weight should be stable. Put the scale on the floor, never on a table. If the guinea pig panics, she can be seriously injured by a fall from the table.

Check the animal's toenails regularly. Overgrown toenails prevent the guinea pig from walking properly and cause her pain. If the nails are too long, they must be trimmed professionally. **2**

3 Inspecting the teeth regularly is a necessary part of guinea pig care. If the animals don't get enough to chew, their teeth grow too long and interfere with eating.

Long-haired guinea pigs require regular grooming with a comb and brush for good hygiene. Smooth-coated animals don't need this type of care, however. **4**

A word of caution, though: Grooming isn't always done for cleanliness' sake. Many animals groom or scratch themselves when they experience conflict. For example, they can't decide if they want to attack an adversary or run away from him. Behavioral scientists call this "displacement behavior." We have identified this type of behavior in guinea pigs, too. They groomed themselves when they were faced with two alternatives in a learning problem or when they didn't know whether to attack a rival or run the other way. We humans behave similarly in conflict situations. For instance, we scratch our heads or we "play" with the pen in our hand. Keep in mind that overgrooming or scratching can also indicate disease such as ectoparasitism.

MY PET

Is your guinea pig maintaining a constant weight?

A guinea pig's weight reveals a lot about its health and well-being. Weight loss can be caused by disease or increased stress. However, stress can also be reflected in weight gain.

The test begins:
Weigh your guinea pig in the pan of a kitchen scale that you have placed on the floor. Make a table using the measurements. Record the animal's starting weight. Does the weight stay constant, or does it change? As a rule of thumb, if a guinea pig loses more than 10 percent of its total weight within three days, you should check to see that there are no social/aggression problems in the group, or else consult the veterinarian.

My test results:

Common Diseases

Guinea pigs are not susceptible to disease, provided they are kept properly. Most ailments are caused by poor husbandry. Of course, your pet may already have been sick when you got him. Here are the most common diseases.

 Guinea pigs seldom get sick. If you watch your animals closely every day, you'll be quick to notice any changes. Don't hesitate to take a sick guinea pig to the veterinarian right away. Guinea pigs, like all small animals, have a high metabolic rate, and germs can spread quickly. Even seemingly mild infections can become life-threatening.

Recognizing Signs of Illness

The following signs can indicate an illness in your guinea pig:
▶ Eating and drinking much less than normal.
▶ Weight loss.
▶ Labored and shallow breathing; runs out of breath quickly.
▶ Persistent discharge from his eyes and/or nose.
▶ Frequent scratching, hair loss, or bald spots.
▶ Persistent digestive problems and diarrhea.
▶ Apathy or lethargy.
My recommendation: Take the guinea pig's temperature. The normal value is 100 to 103.5°F (37.9 to 39.7°C). Use a digital thermometer, because it's easier to read. Smear the tip of the thermometer with a little petroleum jelly and insert it carefully into the anus.
Tip: At the first sign of illness, you should move the little patient into a private cage or a travel carrier although it will increase his stress to be isolated from the group. You must do everything you can to minimize his stress. That move prevents infection of the other guinea pigs and makes it easier to keep an eye on him.

Security When Traveling

The best thing to use for taking your guinea pig to the veterinarian is a plastic travel carrier (from the pet store). A handful of bedding from his cage or pen gives the animal a feeling of security. Try to secure the carrier with a seat belt to minimize movement.

Skin Disorders

Disorders of the skin can have many causes. One common cause is parasites that attack the skin directly. These are called ectoparasites. However, metabolic disorders affecting the internal organs or parasites that live inside the body (= endoparasites) can also cause skin diseases. Infestation with ectoparasites can often be traced to poor husbandry or improper diet. The most common ectoparasites are mites, lice, and fungi.

Mites

These are bad news for our guinea pigs. Mites are arachnids; some, like the mange mite (*Trixacarus caviae*), can burrow directly into the skin. Go to the veterinarian at once, because a severe mite infestation can lead to the death of the animal. Not quite so dangerous is the fur mite. It clings to the hair and feeds on skin secretions. They are found exclusively on the rump and outer thighs.

Symptoms: A mite infestation can create intense inflammation in the skin. Consequently, guinea pigs will scratch and rub, sometimes intensely. Guinea pigs develop flaky skin and scratch wounds.

Possible causes: Mite infestation is frequently an indication of a decreased immune response in the animal. That means you should check the living conditions. Are the animals in the group compatible? Is the cage too small? Are they getting a balanced diet?

Treatment: The veterinarian usually gives the animal an injection to get rid of these parasites. The treatment is generally repeated seven to ten days later. Don't skip the second appointment, even if you have the impression that your guinea pig is doing better. The parasites are stubborn, and some survive a single treatment. Only adult mites are killed by the treatment. Over the next ten to fourteen days, eggs will develop into adults and need to be killed before they lay additional eggs. In chronic cases, the veterinarian prescribes a shampoo to bathe the animal.

If a bath is necessary, I put the guinea pig in a bucket of lukewarm water. She stands on her hind legs while I support her by placing my left hand beneath her front paws. Her head stays above water. I wash her head carefully with the shampoo solution, making sure not to get any in her eyes. Follow the instructions on how long the bath is supposed to last. Too short or too long a time can be harmful for the animal. After the bath, dry your guinea pig gently with a soft towel and protect her from drafts. Now, unfortunately, you have some work in store for you. The cage and surrounding area must be cleaned and disinfected more frequently during treatment. Ask the veterinarian how often you should clean it, which disinfectant you can use, and whether the guinea pig is allowed outdoors. Some veterinarians also recommend that you have the animals sheared to speed up the recovery. Fortunately, my animals have never been infested with these mites, but shearing makes sense.

As for additional medications, a vitamin cocktail in the form of a multivitamin and an increased dose of vitamin C is recommended to strengthen the immune system.

TIP

Finding the right veterinarian

It is not always easy to find a specialist who treats rodents, including guinea pigs. Don't be embarrassed to ask if the veterinarian is experienced with these animals. Contact other guinea pig owners. Inquire about small-animal specialists at the animal shelter. Veterinary schools have rodent specialists on staff and may be able to refer you to a local veterinarian.

The proper way to pick up a guinea pig: Grasp the animal below the chest and support his hindquarters with your other hand.

Tip: Use disposable gloves when giving your guinea pig a medicated bath.

Biting lice

These tiny insects don't burrow into the skin like fleas and sucking lice; instead, they feed on the hair of their host animal. They have three pairs of legs, not four like the mites, and their body is divided into a head, thorax, and abdomen. Biting lice irritate the skin and attach their nits (eggs) to the hair of the guinea pig. These creatures live for about two to three months and usually eat skin scales and exudates like glandular secretions. You can see biting lice with a magnifying glass.

Possible causes: Unfortunately, these parasites are relatively common, so newly purchased animals may already be infested and can then infect your guinea pigs. Objects like brushes and bedding can also be infested. To be on the safe side, you should leave the diagnosis to the veterinarian.

Treatment: The veterinarian will give you a powder or spray that you can use to treat the animal and will explain what you have to do. To get rid of biting lice, you'll need to treat the animals' environment as well.

Prevention: Because lice are a contagious parasite, do not introduce your guinea pig to other guinea pigs of unknown health. All objects that the animals come in contact with must be cleaned as often as possible (at least twice a week). Even the nest box is not exempt.

Tip: I would cut off hair that is especially heavily infested.

Fleas

Guinea pigs suffer less from fleas than do dogs, cats, and rabbits, because there is no host-specific guinea pig flea. That does not mean, though, that fleas of other animal species don't feel right at home on the guinea pig's hide. Even human fleas will hop on guinea pigs.
Treatment: Ask the veterinarian to give you an effective flea control product. Don't forget to treat the guinea pigs' living quarters, too.

Ringworm

Ringworm is a fungal skin infection that also affects people. This stubborn disease is not easy to treat in either us or our guinea pigs.
Symptoms: The symptoms in guinea pigs are severe itching resulting in scratching and biting as well as circular areas of hair loss.
Treatment: Don't delay consulting the veterinarian because the disease can be transmitted to people, particularly those that are immune compromised. A veterinarian is able to make an accurate diagnosis by culturing the fungus.
Tip: Don't let advertisers' claims tempt you to tackle parasites yourself with sprays and solutions. Professional treatment is better and ultimately cheaper.

Ear Disorders

Causes: Fungi, mites, and bacteria can all infect the external ear canal. This can lead to inflammations.
Symptoms: The ear canal is reddened. There is often a brown or black secretion inside. The guinea pig is restless, shakes his head frequently, and tries to scratch himself. An inflammation of the middle ear (otitis media) is more troublesome for the little rodents. It is usu-

ally caused by bacteria. Animals with middle-ear infections are lethargic, don't eat, and have a fever.
Treatment: A veterinarian will discern the precise cause and dispense the appropriate medication for treatment.

Eye Disorders

Eye disorders are relatively rare in guinea pigs. The most common are inflammations of the conjunctiva, eyelids, eyelid margins, and lacrimal glands, because they are relatively unprotected. Guinea pigs have large eyes, but unlike many other animals they do not have a nictitating membrane (third eyelid) to protect the eye from particles of dirt and dust.
Symptoms: Acute conjunctivitis manifests itself as a severe reddening and swelling of the conjunctiva and a viscous ocular discharge.
Possible causes: Drafts, foreign bodies in the eye, and parasites, as well as allergens like pollen.
Treatment: Eye ointment prescribed by the veterinarian.

Cheilitis and Lip Fold Dermatitis

Symptoms: Lips and corners of the mouth are reddened and crusty.
Cause: Develops because of weakened resistance of the skin. Injuries cause microscopic tears in the skin, which are then colonized by bacteria and fungi. The disease is aggravated by deficiencies of unsaturated fatty acids, vitamin A, and vitamin C in the diet.
Treatment: The veterinarian will likely begin with topical ointments or washes and may give systemic antibiotics or antiparasitics as well. For chronic cases, the veterinarian might biopsy or culture

2 **If the anal region** is soiled or caked with feces, you can clean it with a damp cloth as well. A dirty bottom can be a sign of illness.

1 **Watery** and inflamed eyes can be cleaned carefully with a dampened, soft cloth.

3 **Gently clean** the ear flaps. Never push the cloth into the ear canal, though.

the lesions to enhance identification and progress.

Footpad Infection (Bacterial Pododermatitis)

This is usually a very stubborn and protracted ailment.

Symptoms: The pads of the feet are inflamed; in especially severe cases, they can bleed and fester. The animals avoid walking on their infected feet.

Possible cause: Unfortunately, mistakes in feeding and housing are often the cause. A fatty liver and a deficiency in unsaturated fatty acids can be responsible. In addition, cold, damp floors and a lack of exercise frequently lead to an inflammation of the footpads. Overweight animals are especially vulnerable to this problem.

Treatment: Only the veterinarian can help in this case. In addition to recommending changes to the pig's environment, your veterinarian will bandage affected feet, administer antibiotics, and recommend changes and treatment for any underlying conditions.

Diarrhea

Persistent diarrhea can be very dangerous for guinea pigs.

Symptoms: The feces are softer, stickier, and more watery than usual. The anal region and hind legs are soiled with feces. The animal feels sick and lifts its hindquarters noticeably.

Possible causes: Spoiled food and drinking water contaminated with germs like salmonella or *Pasteurella* are frequently responsible. However, you

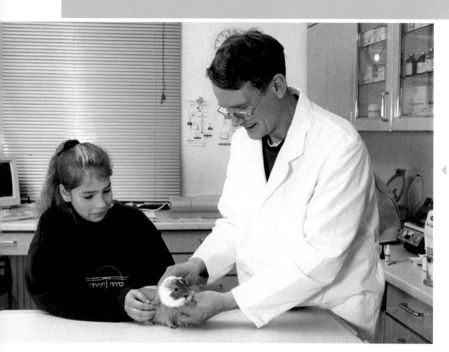

Visiting the veterinarian: A good doctor handles the animal gently and takes his time making a diagnosis. He will explain to you exactly which disease your pet has.

can't rule out fresh foods that don't agree with your pets.

Treatment: Discontinue all fresh foods; instead, feed just hay, crispbread, and slightly sweetened chamomile tea. I put the patient in a spare cage or a large travel carrier to avoid contagion and monitor her better. If the diarrhea doesn't disappear in two days, you should definitely see a veterinarian. The cage must be cleaned with hot water and, after consultation with the veterinarian, treated with a disinfectant solution.

Constipation

Symptoms: The fecal pellets are dry, small, coated with mucus, and hang together. The animals have no appetite and are lethargic.

Possible causes: If fresh water is not always available, guinea pigs can become dehydrated, preventing proper bowel movements. Constipation and impactions can also result from a diet too low in fiber and too high in carbo-

hydrates, a lack of exercise, or misaligned teeth.

Treatment: The recommended treatment is to place the animal on a warm, but not hot, hot-water bottle; a little while later, massage the animal's abdomen by moving two fingers over the left and right sides of the belly with gentle circular motions. Your pig should be offered plenty of fresh water and hay. If the constipation lasts longer than one day, you absolutely must take the animal to the veterinarian.

Heatstroke

Death because of heatstroke is a serious danger for our pets and one that is underestimated by many owners. We humans find this difficult to understand because we can more easily deal with the heat. The evaporation of sweat cools our body. Guinea pigs, however, cannot sweat; they can't even pant the way dogs do. Thus they can't get rid of excess heat. Their only means of escaping the heat is to hide in the shade and to drink water. The problem is even worse for overweight animals. The danger of hyperthermia starts at about 82°F (28°C) with an atmospheric humidity of 70 percent. When transporting your guinea pigs by car, remember that the passenger compartment can heat up quickly, especially in summer. Never leave a pig in a sitting car for even a few minutes on a hot day.

Symptoms: The animals are lethargic, lie on one side, and pant. Their mucous membranes (seen most easily in their mouth) turn gray or blue.

Causes: Exposure to a moderately or highly heated environment without the benefit of shade, a cooling source, and an abundant supply of fresh cool water.

Treatment: If you suspect heatstroke, get the guinea pig to shade or a cool place right away and cool her using cool cloths. Do not place your guinea pig in ice or use ice packs. As a supportive measure, you can also use a fan to blow cool air towards her. As she recovers, allow her to drink cool water. Be careful not to overcool her. If she does not quickly recover, take her to your veterinarian for further emergency treatment.

Colds

Unlike humans, guinea pigs seldom catch colds.

Causes: Drafts and cold floors are conducive to colds.

Symptoms: The guinea pig sneezes, his nose may run, and you can hear whistling noises when he breathes. However, cold-like symptoms may be a sign of an alternate, more serious problem.

Treatment: I recommend infrared light. A heat lamp is beneficial for mild colds

and stimulates both metabolism and circulation. The lamp should shine on only one side of the cage so that the guinea pig can leave the heated area. Obviously, the lamp should not be placed too close to the cage; otherwise

Administering medications

▶ 1 **Liquid medicine** is best given by dropper. Squirt the liquid into the side of your guinea pig's mouth.

▶ 2 **A cotton swab** is helpful when applying an ointment to the skin. Have the veterinarian show you how to administer specific medications to your animal.

you risk hyperthermia! For a stubborn cold, you must consult a veterinarian.

Abscesses and Tumors

If you feel swellings or growths on your pigs' body, have him evaluated by a veterinarian. While these are usually not malignant, they are difficult to differentiate at home and often need to be removed and/or treated.

Abscesses are bacterial infections.
Symptoms: An abscess will appear as any size mass and will sometimes have a purulent foul-smelling discharge.
Cause: Abscesses may be caused by bite wounds. Additionally, if a guinea pig has abrasions in the mouth, bacteria can enter the body and cause abscesses in the lymph nodes in the neck.
Treatment: Antibiotics and surgical removal and drainage of the abscess.

Maggots

Symptoms: You may see wounds on the outside of your guinea pig's body and should be able to see the moving, off-white flea larvae.
Cause: In the summer, flies lay their eggs on damp or dirty spots and wounds on the animal. This could be the animal's soiled anus or else a small cut that has escaped your notice. Within hours, the fly eggs develop into maggots, which then migrate into the guinea pig's body, for instance through the anus, and literally devour the animal from the inside. The only thing the veterinarian can do in this case is euthanize the animal.
Treatment: A guinea pig infested by maggots must be taken immediately to a veterinarian for treatment. Do not delay. The veterinarian will physically remove the maggots—as much as is possible—and treat the underlying disease that drew the fleas in the first place. If the damage is too severe, no treatment will save the guinea pig.

A sick guinea pig needs plenty of rest and close observation. You should look in on him several times a day and check his breathing as well as activity.

Loss of Interest

Our two children have lost all interest in their two guinea pigs. They neglect the animals terribly. They also refuse to clean the cage. We would really like to take the guinea pigs to the animal shelter.

Unfortunately it's not uncommon for children to lose interest in their pets for a while or even altogether. Other activities are frequently to blame, like getting together more often with friends. Nevertheless, you should at least try to reawaken your children's interest in their guinea pigs. Only if all else fails is it time to look for a good home for the animals or, if necessary, take them to the animal shelter.

Keep the lines of communication open

Try to make your children understand how much the animals need their familiar surroundings and how much they suffer when they are passed from hand to hand. Look for convincing comparisons; for example, ask your children how they would feel if they had to move out of their familiar home. Tell them something interesting about the life of the guinea pig, perhaps that their social behavior is fascinating (see page 17) or that guinea pigs are able to fend for themselves almost as soon as they're born. You and your children could carry out one or more of the "My Pet" experiments described in this book and evaluate the results of your observations together. Ask their biology teacher whether it might be possible to have a "pet day" that would motivate the children to give a little talk about their pets. Perhaps you could also allow your children to chat with other guinea pig owners online; there are many interesting home pages and forums devoted to guinea pigs on the Internet.

Firm guidelines

Introduce firm guidelines on who is responsible for taking care of the guinea pigs and when. Together with the children, you can draw up a weekly timetable for all chores, taking into account your children's scheduled activities. Naturally, you must monitor everything conscientiously to make sure that the animals are receiving proper care. Stay in the background, though, so that the children take the lead as responsible "caretakers." Be generous with your praise when the children have carried out their assigned tasks well. I hope you succeed in rekindling their interest with one of these suggestions. But, ultimately, parents must ensure the welfare of pets in their home even if it means providing care themselves.

Activities and Wellness

Life can be very exciting for your pet guinea pigs, provided you give them out-of-cage time and an activity program to prevent boredom.

Keeping Physically and Mentally Fit

Without stimulation and activity, we just waste away. The same is often true for guinea pigs kept as pets. Another guinea pig can help to pass the time, but that alone is not enough. You have to challenge your animals and provide them with stimulating activities.

"Use it or lose it." This motto applies to animals, too, in a figurative sense. Idleness is a luxury few species can afford in the wild. This is especially true of flight animals like guinea pigs. Nature dictates that they must always stay alert to avoid being eaten. Their behavioral repertoire seems to be limited. They are timid and fearful. There is little time left for play in the wild, to say nothing of the fact that it's far too dangerous.

Do Guinea Pigs Play?

Guinea pigs are certainly not the most playful of animals. In comparison to dogs and cats, they play very little. Nevertheless, guinea pigs do play, particularly the youngsters, and I have even seen older animals at play. Castrated animals are an exception: They're extremely playful. They are not as deeply involved in the day-to-day life of the group and have more "free time" because they don't have to worry about choosing a mate or raising young. Why, then, is play so important for humans and animals? Play is training for serious situations later on. This is especially true for animals that don't come into the world with a fully developed pro-

gram of instincts, but instead have to learn about their environment the hard way—through experience. As a rule, the more highly developed and complex an animal's brain, the more the animal has to play when young. During this period, it learns agility, strength, and how to judge members of its group. However, most species play only as youngsters under the watchful eye of their parents. For older animals, this activity is much too risky.

That's because an animal at play forgets itself and its environment and can easily become somebody's dinner, like high-spirited young guinea pigs that

Guinea pigs are clever: With a bit of patience, you can teach them to do little tricks. ▶

Interacting with your guinea pigs **strengthens the bond** between you and the animals. That's why you should take time to play with them.

jump about joyfully, making sudden vertical leaps and twisting around in midair. These agility exercises are necessary for the little rodents, though, so that they will be able to escape their enemies later on. The youngsters also love to play tag; switching back and forth between the hunter and the hunted, they chase each other to the point of exhaustion, then snuggle close together and rest. With many herd animals, mock battles are the order of the day. However, guinea pigs don't play games like this. Their group behavior apparently follows another syllabus. Just recently, behavioral biologists demonstrated that almost all domesticated animals play much longer than their wild relatives. Guinea pigs are most playful in the morning and evening. Tame young guinea pigs like to hop around and chase each other. When they take a break, they will even let you pet them. Familiar sounds like squeaking and

cooing make guinea pigs feel secure and encourage them to play.

It Mustn't Get Boring

Life in the wild cannot be compared with life in the care of humans. Our pet guinea pigs are largely protected from their enemies, and must not constantly search for food. What's left is plenty of time. Guinea pigs without companions don't know what to do with themselves and in some cases are bored. Animals living in a group are much better off. They can communicate with their partners. In my opinion, though, that is by no means enough. Domestic animals need lots of activities as a substitute for life in the wild. These activities can be of all kinds, from searching for hidden food to solving puzzles. Naturally, not all species can be judged according to the same standard. Their talents and mental abilities vary greatly. Because of

It's up and over the box for a tasty treat.
▼

their fearful and timid nature, guinea pigs are often misjudged. They are regarded as sweet, but not very bright. Take away their natural timidity, though, and you'll find that this is merely prejudice.

Guinea pigs love to go exploring. They sniff at everything they come across and give every object a once-over with their incisors. An elevated perch lets them observe their surroundings. You can even teach them little tricks if you do it with kindness. Training

Creating the right conditions

As a rule, guinea pigs need a relaxed environment. What does that mean? Don't practice with your animals when you can hear loud, high-frequency noises in the vicinity (for example, construction work). The noise makes the guinea pigs anxious. Avoid very bright light. Punishment is forbidden; only praise will do. Guinea pigs are easily

DID YOU KNOW THAT . . .

. . . guinea pigs are misunderstood?

Guinea pigs learn well only if the conditions are right. When they feel anxious and stressed, they refuse to cooperate. Scientists were astonished to find that they did just as well in tests as rats, which are considered highly intelligent rodents. If food was hidden from the guinea pigs at various locations and they were given different amounts of food at each place, they quickly learned where to run.

guinea pigs can enhance their safety and interest in the environment as well as further bond your relationship so long as it is done properly and with respect for your pet. Scientists have found that the nerve cells in the guinea pig's brain form many more connections when the animals live in an exciting environment. The circuitry in the brain becomes more complex and consequently more efficient. Guinea pigs should be stimulated and challenged. That contributes to their well-being.

tempted with a treat; we have often encouraged them this way, and they always enjoyed it. The little rodents are more attentive if you teach them individually; in a group, they are too easily distracted. Guinea pigs learn very quickly at nine to ten months of age. This came as a surprise to us, because it's relatively late in comparison to other animals with a longer life expectancy, like dogs and cats. Younger animals are still too timid. The animals learn more easily in familiar surroundings where they feel safe and are ready to try some-

Exercise Course

▶ **1** **A chew tree** like this keeps them fit. The guinea pig really has to stretch to reach the coveted treat.

▶ **2** **Agility exercises,** like balancing on the see-saw here, are also a part of the exercise program.

▶ **3** **An obstacle course** made from branches is good for the figure. This exercise is not easy for a guinea pig.

thing new. Everything runs smoothly if the smell is right, so rub your hands with bedding from the cage before each training session. Some of the critters in our experiments could scarcely wait to tackle another problem. I now know how important activity is for guinea pigs. Unfortunately, in practice it's usually difficult to spend a lot of time with the little fellows. At any rate, though, an exercise area or a "playpen" with a variety of activities (see page 39) or an attractively designed outdoor enclosure will help counteract boredom. This keeps the animals mentally and physically fit. You can let your imagination run wild when it comes to furnishing the "playpen" and outdoor enclosure. There are many ways to provide a little variety for your animals (see page 103).

Guinea Pig Learning

Guinea pigs easily identify voices.
Recognizing voices: To perform a simple survey test, four different people called to my guinea pigs. When I did it, they came running up right away and got a carrot. When my friend tried, they hesitated a little at first and then came; they didn't come at all for my two children, who no longer live at home. They recognized my wife's voice immediately. We tested this again with other groups, always with the same result. These findings agree with the observations of many guinea pig owners. Some guinea pigs even squeal for joy when the familiar car drives up.

A little "trick": One trick my guinea pigs learned was to run to the right-hand corner of the cage when they heard a low note and to the left corner at a higher-pitched one. How do you manage that? It's easy. If the guinea pig runs to the right when he hears a low note, he gets a little piece of carrot; if he goes the wrong way, he gets nothing. After a few unsuccessful attempts, he will have learned the task. No one can become a master overnight, not even a guinea pig. Try this little "training exer-

cise" again and again. One day, he'll finally catch on.

Learning names: I'm often asked if guinea pigs can learn their names. To be honest, I'm not really sure, although I did teach each of my animals its own name. This is how it works: Put your little student in front of you on the floor, show him the reward (for example, a carrot) in your hand, and call him by name. A tame animal won't be able to resist this temptation and will hurry over. Repeat the activity several times and finally perform the acid test without a carrot—just call his name. The guinea pig will come trotting up happily like a good little fellow. But there's no cause to celebrate just yet, because you don't know if he has learned the sound or the name. One argument against it is this: When I called one of my bunch, usually all of them came. Sometimes I had the impression that the one I called reacted more quickly, but I have never tested it scientifically.

Good sense of direction: Guinea pigs quickly learn to find their way through passageways. We built them a Y-shaped system of corridors using planks or bricks. The two corridors—both sides of the Y—were different: One was dark, the other light. We covered the walls of one corridor with black paper and the other with white paper. The guinea pigs' task was to collect a reward at the end of the light-colored passageway.

TIP

Easy to clean!

Homemade or store-bought toys must be easy to clean, because guinea pigs soil them quickly with urine and feces. Make sure that you can scrub the objects under hot water from time to time without any difficulty. Afterward dry everything thoroughly.

After four or five tries, the animals had learned that food was to be found only in the light corridor. They had no difficulty, even when we switched the passageways. The guinea pigs knew that only the light one had food, regardless of where it led. A little story illustrates how clever guinea pigs are. One test subject chose the dark corridor and didn't notice his mistake until he was halfway through. Without further ado, he jumped over the wall into the other corridor and collected his reward. You can even expand the corridor system into a labyrinth; guinea pigs will find their way through it without much effort. In our experiments, they immediately located the exit in a difficult maze without getting lost.

Pressing keys: Guinea pigs can also learn to push colored keys, for example, those on a small toy keyboard. How can you teach your guinea pig to do this? It's very easy: Place a piece of carrot on the key; the guinea pig will immediately come up to the key and press it inadvertently. Repeat this a few times. Now what had been accidental becomes deliberate. Don't put any more carrots on the key; instead, wait until the animal presses the key impatiently. That's when you give him the carrot. After a few times the animal will understand the connection—press a key and get food.

We were surprised at how quickly the guinea pigs learned this. They were no slower than rats. Our experiments were actually a preliminary step in testing whether guinea pigs can see colors, but we were also quite impressed by their ability to remember. Even after more than a year, they still knew how to work the keys and press experimental levers to get what they wanted. As you can see, guinea pigs are not dumb.

Recognizing shapes: Guinea pigs also learn relatively quickly to distinguish a rectangle from a triangle. The same method is used here. The animal gets a reward only by going to the food bowl on which you have drawn a circle, rectangle, or triangle with a black marker.

◀ *Rock climbing in the outdoor pen is fun. Natural materials like rocks, branches, and roots provide a welcome diversion.*

Variety in the Guinea Pigs' Life

Activity is everything in the lives of our pet guinea pigs, so here are a few practical ideas on providing it. Well-known animal photographer and author Monika Wegler developed a chew tree, some steps, a seesaw, and a little obstacle course for her guinea pigs. Except for the steps, all of this "exercise equipment" is made of untreated wood so that the animals can also safely gnaw on it. Try your hand at building them. Your guinea pigs will thank you for it.

The chew tree

The chew tree encourages your guinea pigs to work for their food. You can easily build one like it (see photo, page 100).

You need: A forked branch with bark or a squared timber about 12 inches (30 cm) long and 6 inches (15 cm) in diameter, a round or rectangular plywood base with a diameter of about 16 inches (40 cm), two or three long wood screws, and a wood drill.

How to make it: Bore holes at various heights in the upper part of the branch or timber, starting about 5 inches (12 cm) from the bottom.

Then screw the branch or timber to the base, and the chew tree is finished. Now decorate the tree with a variety of healthy treats, such as carrots, parsley, and dandelions. You'll see how eagerly your pets stretch to get them.

Seesaw

This develops your pets' sense of balance. It is important that the seesaw descend slowly when the animals run across it. Naturally, a treat provides extra motivation here, as always. It's

---

CHECKLIST

Hazards

Guinea pigs need lots of exercise. That's why daily out-of-cage time is a must. Remove any possible hazards beforehand, though, or take the necessary precautions.

- ○ Don't leave pointed objects like needles or thumbtacks lying around.

- ○ Remove sharp objects like knives.

- ○ Move poisonous houseplants out of reach (see page 75). If the animals nibble on them, they can be poisoned.

- ○ Open and close doors carefully so an animal doesn't get caught.

- ○ Don't put the animal on the table.

- ○ Be careful not to step on an animal by accident.

- ○ Lock up household cleaning products.

- ○ Put electrical cords where the animals can't get to them, for instance, under the rug or behind strips of molding.

- ○ Cover balcony railings with wire mesh or barrier netting.

- ○ Guinea pigs are very susceptible to heatstroke, so always provide shade (see page 92).

MY PET

Can guinea pigs tell people apart?

Guinea pigs can differentiate a variety of sounds, tones, and voices; presumably they can also recognize different humans. Carry out a little test to find out if it's true.

The test begins:

You must have a partner for this test. The guinea pig should know the other person. Place yourselves at opposite corners of the outdoor pen. Both of you call the guinea pig, but only one person gives the animal a piece of carrot. Naturally, she will run to you in the beginning. Feed her the first time so that she's not disappointed, but after that only your partner gives her food. Switch places occasionally.

My test results:

easy to make "exercise equipment" like this yourself (see photo, page 101).
You need: A log about $6\frac{1}{2}$ inches (16 cm) long and about 5 inches (12 cm) in diameter; a plank about $\frac{3}{4}$ inch (2 cm) thick, $5\frac{1}{2}$ inches (14 cm) wide, and 26 inches (65 cm) long; nine thin branches, each about $5\frac{1}{2}$ inches (14 cm) long; two long wood screws; two small screws for each branch; a saw and a screwdriver.
How to make it: Screw the branches to the plank at intervals of about 2 inches (5 cm). They will prevent the guinea pig from slipping off as she runs over the board. Now flatten one side of the log by sawing it lengthwise to remove about one-third of the diameter. Finally, screw the plank to the flattened side of the log. Your seesaw is finished!

Obstacle Course

Exercise is important for guinea pigs, so here's the description of an obstacle course (see photo, page 101).
You need: A board 28 inches (70 cm) long and $5\frac{1}{2}$ inches (14 cm) wide as the base, four branches about $1\frac{1}{2}$ inches (4 cm) in diameter and $9\frac{1}{2}$ inches (24 cm) long, wood screws, and a screwdriver.
How to make it: Simply screw the branches to the base at intervals of about 5 inches (13 cm), and you have an obstacle course. Use a treat to encourage your guinea pig to run through the course, perhaps a sprig of parsley.

"Stairway to heaven"

You can make some steps using auto-claved aerated concrete, also called air-crete (available at home-improvement centers). They will keep your guinea pigs on the move while providing a lookout tower and a great spot for sun-bathing (in the outdoor enclosure).

You need: Three aircrete blocks of different sizes; the largest block, about 2¾ inches (7 cm) thick, forms the base. Paint, paintbrush.

How to make it: Cut the blocks to the desired size using a saw. Smooth any sharp edges with a wood file. Since the material crumbles, you should paint the blocks with nontoxic paint. Then stack up the blocks, and you're finished! Make sure that the steps are stable.

More Ideas for Activities

Hurdles: Guinea pigs quickly learn to jump over hurdles, especially if there's a tempting reward on the other side. Naturally, the hurdle shouldn't be too high; 4 inches (10 cm) is high enough to start with.

Woven-grass hideaways: Hideaways like this are available at pet supply stores. The animals can crawl through them. Make the nest even more attractive by rubbing the inside with bedding from the cage.

Hunting for food: Hide treats (like bits of carrot) at different places in the outdoor pen. Searching for food is entertaining and good exercise.

Tube mazes: Use cardboard tubes as barriers or as tunnels. That arouses the animals' curiosity. You can even use the tubes to make actual mazes.

The guinea pig has to "work" for the lettuce in the ball. It's fun and good exercise.

Questions About
Activities and Wellness

? Why does my guinea pig suddenly freeze for no apparent reason?

When a guinea pig suddenly stands absolutely still, there is always a reason. The technical term for this behavior is "freezing." The animal has probably heard something that frightened it, although the sound may be inaudible to us. Freezing is the typical reaction to this. Guinea pigs are able to hear high-pitched sounds in particular better than we can.

? I think one of my guinea pigs is more intelligent than the other. Is that possible?

In numerous experiments on learning ability, I have found that there actually are differences. However, you should be careful about making sweeping generalizations on intelligence in animals. Like us, their strengths lie in different areas. For instance, some of my guinea pigs quickly learned how to push a lever, whereas others turned out to be true masters at navigating mazes and never lost their way, even in very complex labyrinths. Surprisingly, my castrated males were often better at problem-solving.

? At what age do guinea pigs actually stop playing?

As a rule, playfulness declines sharply after sexual maturity in animals, including guinea pigs, which are sexually mature at just a few weeks of age. With enough encouragement, though, the older ones will still play on occasion. It has been shown that domestic animals play longer than wild animals. In the wild, most animal species play only as youngsters under the watchful eye of their parents. For older animals, this activity is much too risky. In play, an animal forgets itself and its environment all too easily and can quickly become prey.

? My guinea pigs have a large outdoor enclosure. Unfortunately, they don't use it but stay inside their shelter instead!

That is unusual and leads me to suspect that your animals are afraid of something. You can test this: Place the enclosure in a different spot and provide the animals with some interesting toys, such as a bridge to run over or a cork tube to crawl through. Scatter a variety of treats around the pen. Hang a little bunch of tasty herbs on the fence of the enclosure so that your guinea pigs have to stretch to reach it. Are they still hesitant to come out? If so, a neighbor's dog or cat may be the reason for their fear.

? Is it unnatural to teach a guinea pig to stand on her hind legs?

Not at all. Physical and mental activities are good for your animal in any case. As with any good training, an exercise like this only

develops a natural ability that is already present. Standing on their hind legs is part of the guinea pigs' innate behavioral repertoire. Even in the wild, they stand on their hind legs to reach something, for instance, food in a bush. Here's how your guinea pig learns fastest: Hold a carrot in front of the animal's nose and slowly raise it higher. The guinea pig will try to snatch the treat and will finally stand on her hind legs briefly. When she succeeds, give her lots of praise and, naturally, the juicy carrot as a reward.

? My son is eight years old, and he's trying to train his guinea pigs. Is he too young to do this?

There are always children with a special gift. They can put themselves in the animal's place and feel intuitively what the animal wants and what it intends. This leads to the development of a close relationship that promotes learning. Guinea pigs are placid, patient animals. That makes it easier to deal with them, and you need have no fear that your son will get hurt. Nevertheless, keep an eye on both the boy and the guinea pig, because children are sometimes unintentionally rough with animals. That's when the guinea pigs' peaceful nature can be their undoing. They can't express their annoyance by biting or growling. To be on the safe side, demonstrate how to treat the animals carefully and gently. Show your son how to hold them securely and when to let them rest for a bit. Once he understands that, nothing will hinder him from training his pets.

? My two guinea pigs are rather sluggish and lazy. What can I do to remedy this?

With guinea pigs, as with all animals, there are different temperaments. However, laziness cannot be allowed to go too far. It's bad for the animals' health because too little exercise leads to obesity. What can you do, then? Every day, encourage your animals to do something to get a tasty bit of food. Raise the food bowl slightly, perhaps by placing it on a wooden bridge where the animals have to jump up or walk to reach it, or else scatter the food around the outdoor enclosure. Let your motto be "Encourage activity."

7 Family Planning

Baby guinea pigs are adorable, and guinea pigs are very fertile. But what will you do with all the youngsters? Before you start, think about whether you will be able to find good homes for all of them.

How Males and Females Mate

Responsible guinea pig owners don't try to have their animals reproduce like they would in the "wild." You have to plan for healthy guinea pig offspring, and this requires some preparation.

Without a doubt, it's exciting to witness every aspect of guinea pig biology, including mating, pregnancy, birth, and raising the young (pups). But before you embark on this adventure, you have a few things to consider and to plan.

What to Do with the Offspring?

As an animal lover and guinea pig friend, you are certainly concerned about the welfare of your animals. Before you start breeding your pets, remember that guinea pigs can have lots of offspring (see page 114). All too often, youngsters wind up with owners who can't provide adequate living conditions. If the little ones are lucky, they'll find a place in an animal shelter where they will receive proper care. However, the animal shelter should be only a stopover and not a permanent home. Don't shift your responsibility for the animals to an institution whose goal is to help animals in need. That's expecting too much of the shelter. You must assume the responsibility yourself and breed your animals only if you know how and where their offspring will live. If the baby guinea pigs are to

remain with you, make sure you have enough room. You could suddenly find yourself with three or four more animals. That's not just a question of space, but could also be a problem for the herd. If the young guinea pigs are males, they will have difficulty integrating themselves. Then you might have to give the pups away or have them castrated (see page 115). Think carefully about whether you want to tackle these problems. If you have found a new home for your offspring, make sure that the new owners will assume full responsibility for their charges. You have to be certain prospective owners aren't acting

This very ▶
pregnant female
will soon give
birth to her pups.
Right now, she
needs lots of rest.

on impulse or because their children are pressuring them. I give my pups only to private individuals, because then I know exactly where my guinea pigs will be living. I refuse to give them to a pet store. It's not that the animals wouldn't do well there, but pet stores are only temporary quarters. The young guinea pigs would then have three homes in rapid succession, moving

Healthy Parents

Once you have arranged for homes for the pups, check to be sure the future parents are suitable for breeding. It takes a lot of energy to bring baby guinea pigs into the world, and therefore it is imperative that the parents be healthy and active.

Weight monitoring: Your guinea pigs' weight reveals a lot about their state of health. Check to see if the animals' weight remains constant over two or

DID YOU KNOW THAT . . .

. . . females have a vaginal closure membrane?

In many animal species, the vagina is closed by a membrane until the first copulation, and then it remains open. In guinea pigs, it is open only during estrus and then closes again afterward. One of the functions of the vaginal closure membrane is to protect the young animal from the entry of pathogenic organisms. There is less danger of this later because the pathogens are flushed out.

from their birthplace to the pet store and then into a new home. I would like to spare my sensitive little creatures this experience. Sometimes small zoos are grateful for the pups. They need young animals to prevent inbreeding. Check to see that the compound meets your requirements. If it does, then this is a good place for your guinea pig's offspring. Obtain a guarantee of the guinea pig's future living conditions.

three weeks (see page 86). Males should weigh at least 17 ounces (500 g), females at least 24 ounces (700 g). Pregnancy is risky for obese females weighing more than 35 ounces (1,000 g), so I wouldn't breed them.

Breeding age: The age of the guinea pigs plays an important role as well. Females should be mated for the first time when they are five to six months old. The female should be no more than eight to twelve months old when she delivers her first litter. The interval between additional litters should be not

You get healthy guinea pig offspring only with **healthy parents**. Make certain you pay attention to this when choosing the breeding animals.

much more than seven months; otherwise there is a danger that her pelvic bones will fuse (see page 114). Males should not be bred until they are six to seven months old.

Hereditary diseases: Like all creatures, guinea pigs suffer from diseases that are genetic in origin. What we are and what we will become is largely encoded in our DNA, the molecule that is the basis of heredity. It can be compared to a computer program containing highly specific information. What makes our hand have five fingers is information stored in our DNA. It's rare for a person to have six fingers. When it happens, though, it's because their DNA was altered and along with it their genetic information. You can compare it to a typing error in a word processing program. For example, the word "house" becomes "louse" or "mouse"; similarly, altering just one letter in the genetic program can result in major changes. Hereditary diseases, then, are caused by changes in the information stored in the DNA and are passed on from generation to generation. Many such diseases are known in humans; they occur in guinea pigs as well. If one of your guinea pigs has a deformity like misaligned teeth, the wrong number of claws, or some other genetic defect, then under no circumstance should you breed this animal.

The lethal gene: I must warn you against breeding roan or Dalmatian guinea pigs. These animals carry a so-called lethal gene that causes deformities and stillbirths. The only way to be certain that a guinea pig doesn't carry this gene is to analyze the animal's pedigree. If there is no increased rate of mortality and deformities in the animal's family tree (grandparents, great-grandparents, and so on), you can be almost certain that this animal does not carry the gene. Good pet stores and breeders make sure that their animals aren't carrying a hidden copy of this gene.

These three-day-old youngsters look almost like full-grown animals.
▼

Heredity: How are traits and characteristics inherited? In all higher forms of life, the genetic information is present in duplicate in the cells and is passed on by the father and mother. The genes are on the chromosomes. These are like the quipu of the ancient Incas, knotted strings used to carry messages; the "knot words" are the genes. Not all genes are equal, though; some (called dominant) can mask others (called recessive). In our case, the gene for roan coat color and the lethal gene lie on the same chromosome. The roan and related Dalmatian patterns are inherited as dominant traits. An animal that carries one dominant and one recessive roan gene (heterozygous) is healthy; animals like this clearly display the roan or Dalmatian coat pattern. If the animal has two recessive genes (homozygous recessive), it is a solid color and healthy. An unfortunate animal with two dominant genes (homozygous dominant) is sickly and often deformed. Do not attempt to breed roan and/or Dalmatian guinea pigs. The only way to prevent them from having offspring is to neuter them (see page 115).

The Art of Being Born

I have lived through many guinea pig births at the crack of dawn and in the middle of the night, but mother or babies never seemed to have any difficulties. That's amazing, because guinea pigs are almost fully developed at birth. They are covered with hair, have a full set of teeth, and can see. Although lightweights in comparison to the mother, they still weigh in at 2 to $2\frac{3}{4}$ ounces (60 to 80 g). As a rule, the more highly developed an animal is at birth,

the more difficult the delivery. In this respect, their relatives, rats and mice, have an easier time of it. They give birth to blind, naked babies, but then the real work begins for the mother mouse or rat as she tries to feed the hungry mouths. The guinea pig mother already has most of it behind her (see Pregnancy, page 113). Up to that point, though, there is a lot involved in producing the next generation.

Courtship and Mating

Guinea pig males are persistent suitors. Once they've caught the scent of their beloved, almost nothing can deflect them from their objective. If the male is too pushy and the female is still not in the mood, she tries to fend him off by kicking out at him with her hind legs. If that doesn't work, she suddenly lifts her hindquarters as far as possible and shoots a jet of urine almost horizontally toward the rear. For the moment, that is an effective method of defense.

TIP

How to tell if a female is pregnant

Fourteen days after copulation, you can no longer miss the female's plump belly. The scale also tells you that she is pregnant. Be careful weighing her (see page 86)! Six to seven weeks before the birth, her nipples also begin to swell.

When you're little, every-thing you find is exciting. ▶

Mating ritual: If the female is willing, however, the male sniffs at her nose, then usually bows and sniffs her flanks, back, the sides of her head, and finally her genitals. He circles the female in slow motion and makes a low sound: He purrs at her. If she remains sitting, he continues to circle her and at brief intervals lowers his testicles. If the courtship is successful, the male tries to mount her.

Mating: The female shows her willingness by lifting her hindquarters and displaying her genitals. Copulation lasts about fifteen to thirty seconds. Afterward, each one licks its genitals. Following a pause of at least a minute, they begin to mate again. To be certain that only his genes are passed on to the next generation, the male closes the female's vagina with a copulatory plug, which falls out a few hours later. Now it is clear that he will be the actual father.

Pregnancy

A guinea pig pregnancy lasts an average of 63 days with a range from 59 to 72 days. A few figures can make this clear: A guinea pig pup weighs about 2 to $2\frac{3}{4}$ ounces (60 to 80 g) at birth; a mother with three babies is carrying more than 6 ounces (180 grams), not much of it maternal tissues. That's a huge amount. It represents approximately one-third of her body weight.

Feeding pregnant females: During pregnancy the female needs at least 20 mg/day of vitamin C as well as more pellets and fresh foods. The pregnant female will let you know just how much more by immediately devouring everything you put in her bowl. Unfortunately, it's impossible to be any more precise because it all depends on the mother's metabolism and the number of babies. Don't worry; you'll understand your pet's signals.

Feeling the young: After just four weeks of pregnancy, you can feel the young by gently palpating the mother's abdomen. At seven weeks you can detect their movements. Caution! Be very careful when picking up the pregnant female, and do so only when it's absolutely necessary. If you are overcome by curiosity and can't resist feeling the babies inside the mother's body, then I recommend the following: Touch her belly carefully with your index finger and stroke it while she is eating. Don't press too hard!

What the baby experiences in the womb: We still aren't certain, but thanks to Sylvia Kaiser of Norbert Sachser's team, we are much closer to understanding the secret. Her discovery is also of practical use for owners. She found that daughters of guinea pig mothers that lived in an unstable environment displayed masculine characteristics. An unstable environment is one in which the animals often changed groups. The daughters acted macho and exhibited male courtship behavior. Like their male colleagues, they were more aggressive toward the other members of their herd. To avoid getting a troublesome female, ask the owner how and where the pregnant mother lived.

Birth

The behavior of the female reveals very little about the delivery date. Many other rodents build a nest or dig a burrow, indicating that birth is imminent, but not guinea pigs. That's why you don't need to set up a special box where your pregnant sow can give birth to her litter; a large, roomy cage is adequate.

In fact, guinea pigs don't make it easy to determine when the pups are due. Only the expansion of the pelvic girdle lets you guess the approximate date. There is a gap between the pelvic bones called the pelvic symphysis. This gap is held together by ligaments and can expand as much as $\frac{1}{2}$ to $\frac{3}{4}$ inch (1.5 to 2 cm) shortly before birth. This separa-

tion of the pelvis, which seems to be unique in the animal kingdom, can spell disaster for mother and babies. If a first-time mother is more than ten or eleven months old, the ligaments may not be elastic enough or the symphysis may be calcified. This is fatal for the mother. That's why you should always breed your female guinea pigs when they are young, and never later than eight to twelve months of age (see page 111).

Labor and delivery: About 20 minutes before delivery, the contractions begin. The female gives birth in a squatting position, her hind legs spread apart. The baby appears head first. The mother pulls the newborn from beneath her belly, between her hind and front legs, and frees it from the fetal membranes. Then she licks it clean. If the father is there, he often helps to clean the babies.

Now it's time to separate the parents, because $1\frac{1}{2}$ to 13 hours after birth, the female will be in heat again.

Litter size: How many pups a guinea pig has depends heavily on the physical condition and age of the mother. The average litter size is 3 pups. There would be considerably more if 25 percent of the embryos didn't die in utero. The dead embryos do not represent much of a danger for the mother.

Tip: First-time mothers usually have only one or two pups. This is nature's grace period, but things change with the following litters. It's not uncommon for females to bear litters of four and sometimes even more pups.

From their very first day, little guinea pigs eat dry food.

Rest period between litters: Give your female guinea pigs a respite between litters. That's good for them. Your guinea pigs should not have more than one or at most two litters a year. The female usually comes into heat every 18 days.

Neutering

Without a doubt, this is a drastic intervention in the guinea pig's life. In males, the testicles are removed (castration) and the body no longer produces the male hormone testosterone. As a rule, this affects the males' behavior, often turning quarrelsome ruffians into placid members of the herd. However, the primary goal of castration is to prevent offspring. Although the pros and cons of castration are hotly debated, I

believe it is justifiable in order to avoid litter after litter of guinea pig babies. Neutering of the females, called spaying, requires the removal of the ovaries; medically it is more difficult and involves more risk than castration of the males. If you have decided that your guinea pigs shouldn't have any more offspring, then look for an experienced veterinarian, because expertise is required for the surgery and proper administration of anesthesia. As a rule, the patient usually stays at the veterinarian's until he/she wakes up. Once your guinea pig is home, cover the floor of the cage with towels to prevent the incision from being contaminated by bedding. To make certain there are no unexpected offspring, you still have to keep the castrated male separated from the female for another six weeks. Sperm can remain in the urogenital tract during that time.

Youngsters look like miniature versions of adult guinea pigs. Right after birth, they leave the nest and explore their surroundings.

▼

Development of the Young

Young guinea pigs are almost fully developed at birth. Nevertheless, they still have to learn how to make their way in life. Being able to help them along and watch them grow makes rearing the young especially interesting.

Guinea pigs are accused of being neglectful mothers, but that's not true. Admittedly, the guinea pig mother doesn't invest nearly as much effort as a mother rat or mouse, but that's because her young were already well developed when they were born (see page 112).

The First Four Weeks

Right after birth, the babies clean themselves; it's no wonder, then, that you seldom see how the mother licks them clean. The young are nursed until they are 19 to 28 days old.

The mother has two nipples in the groin area. Far too few, you would think, if there are four pups in the litter; two must always lose out. This doesn't play a major role with guinea pigs, though, because they eat solid food from the very first day. While two are nursing at their mother's breast, the others are devouring their first greens. It is ideal when other mothers of the same herd have offspring at about the same time. Then the little ones can choose freely where they want to nurse. If their mother's nipples are occupied, they can try their luck with their aunt next door. Of course, that works only because guinea pig mothers will allow other females' pups to nurse, provided

the pups are from their own clan. Pups of mothers belonging to another herd are chased away, even if the little ones have had the cage odor rubbed into their fur. Apparently the mothers have no trouble telling the difference between youngsters of their own herd and those of a different one.

After about 21 to 30 days, the mother's "milk bar" closes. The youngsters now weigh about 5½ ounces (160 g) and are on their own. At this point, the mother's milk flow dries up.

> **TIP**
>
> ### Separating the family
>
> Females are already sexually mature at three to five weeks of age, males at seven to eight weeks. That's why you should separate the parents as well as the siblings at the appropriate time in order to avoid additional offspring. Castrating the male helps (see page 115).

If the mother is tame, she will allow you to handle her pups.

"Teenagers"

What do the youngsters do between birth and independence? What all children do—they play. Their favorite game is "popcorning," in which the youngster jumps through the room in short, exaggerated hops or makes sudden vertical leaps and midair turns.

The siblings have close contact with each other. They use so-called contact calls to reassure themselves of each other's presence. Animals of the same age form regular little bands that always stay close to each other and even sleep and rest huddled together. If you give the offspring a choice between their mother and the herd, they prefer the latter.

And what is the mother doing now? She's busy keeping an eye on her pups. If the youngsters squeal, she comes running up. Cries of fear trigger alarm in her. She drops everything and hurries to her pup. She even boxes away males

that are bothering the youngsters. Behavioral biologists Peter and Irene Kunkel observed how one mother boxed away a Syrian hamster when he bit one of her babies. You would think this is only natural, but that's not the case with guinea pigs. The little rodents have an inhibition toward biting animals of other species. This is the result of centuries of breeding. However, their wild cousins bite, and they aren't shy about it.

Mother and pups stick together. After a lengthy separation, they greet each other by sniffing noses at length. Guinea pigs have a brief childhood. It takes just a few weeks to go from infancy to adulthood.

Sexual maturity: Males reach sexual maturity between the sixth and tenth week, and by $2\frac{1}{2}$ months of age they are ready to breed. Females ovulate for the first time at just four weeks of age, and their first mating should take place before they are 12 months old (see page 111).

Raising Guinea Pigs by Hand

Raising guinea pigs by hand is easy compared with other animal species because they are almost fully developed at birth and can eat on their own soon after. However, that depends on them having received some of mom's colostrum prior to requiring hand feeding. Pups that haven't received colostrum are unlikely to survive. Nevertheless, the young need a substitute for their mother's milk during the first weeks of life. The following mixture is recommended as a milk replacement: 25 ounces (700 g) cow's milk; $1\frac{3}{4}$

Development of the Young
at a Glance

Guinea pig companions

Even in the first hours of life, other guinea pigs are very important for the youngster. They give him a sense of security, and the little one starts to learn the rules of the herd right away.

◀ The first hours

After the mother has freed the newborn from the fetal membranes and licked him dry, the pup goes exploring for the first time. All of his senses are fully developed by now.

◀ Mother and baby

There is a close relationship between the mother and her pups. They use contact calls to let each other know their whereabouts. If the mother is too far away, the little one gets her attention by squealing.

Eating on its own ▶

Although the pups still nurse, they can now eat on their own. Mother's milk alone is not enough to satisfy the energy requirements of the youngsters.

Playing

Even shortly after birth, young guinea pigs play a lot. One of their favorite games is "popcorning." This way they exercise their muscles and develop agility.

ounces (50 g) egg yolk; 5¼ ounces (150 g) cream with 30 percent fat; 1¾ ounces (50 g) sunflower oil; ¾ ounce (20 g) of a vitamin and mineral mixture; and some vitamin C. Alternatively, you can use dog milk replacer or pellets soaked in Esbilac (dog milk replacer). It's best to give the little ones milk replacement two or three times a day. Depending on how hungry they are, give them ¼ to ¾ ounce (5 to 20 g). This energy-rich liquid diet is important because the babies are already very active. They can already move freely and maintain a constant body temperature of about 100°F (38°C). To spare yourself unnecessary work, divide the mixture into several small portions and freeze them. When you need some, warm up an individual portion to body temperature and feed it to the pups.

How do you feed the babies?

Guinea pigs can drink out of a shallow bowl just a few hours after birth. But even at this young age, guinea pigs are often individualists and some of them turn their nose up at the bowl. Then what? In this case, your only option is to force-feed them with a dropper. You can get droppers like this at a pet store or pharmacy. Proceed carefully when feeding. It's best if you have a helper. One person holds the baby and the

MY PET

Are guinea pigs negligent mothers?

Guinea pig pups come into the world almost fully developed. Does this mean that the mother devotes little attention to her babies? Take a look at maternal love in guinea pigs.

The test begins:

Note down all the behaviors of the mother and her young over the space of an hour. Observe how much time mother and babies spend together, how often she cleans them with her tongue, and whether she shows favoritism toward any of them. Remove one of the babies from the cage and make a note of whether the two call to each other. Now, are you disappointed or instead surprised at everything guinea pig mothers do for their offspring?

My test results:

At six weeks of age, the little guinea pigs can be placed in good homes.

other carefully feeds it small sips of milk. This minimizes the risk of choking.

Time to Give Them Away

There are different opinions on this subject. One side argues in favor of an early date—one week or so after birth—so that the youngsters can acclimate quickly. The other, to which I belong, prefers to give them away later on. Childhood plays a major role in the life of a guinea pig. This is when pups learn the rules of the herd and how to behave in the group. In short, they learn self-assessment of their role (see page 19). I am convinced that this experience contributes to the well-being of the animals. I don't give away my pups until two weeks after they have stopped nurs-

ing. I've found that this works well. Perhaps animals like this are somewhat more difficult to tame, but the advantages outweigh the disadvantages. None of my animals are prone to behavioral problems. You should spend a lot of time interacting with the youngsters. I start taming the pups while they are still living in the herd. I teach them to eat treats from my hand and get them used to the human scent and voice by picking them up in my arms four or five times a day, petting them, and talking to them. This affectionate interaction should not last longer than five to seven minutes.

What to Do When There Are Problems?

Even when keeping peaceable guinea pigs, problems can arise. In most cases, these can be traced to improper handling or poor husbandry.

Solving Husbandry Problems the Right Way

If you have learned as much as you can about the nature and needs of guinea pigs, there's really not much that can go wrong. Sometimes, though, you're suddenly faced with a problem. In this chapter, you can learn how to solve it.

By now it's apparent why guinea pigs are such popular pets. Most problems that arise when keeping them can be solved quickly with a bit of understanding and love. I know of few animals that are so immune to behavioral problems. Their Achilles heel is their susceptibility to stress and herd composition. A world entirely without problems does not exist, though, not even for guinea pigs.

When the Guinea Pig's Partner Dies

Even among guinea pigs, the partner can die prematurely. If the animals live in a small herd, this isn't too great a problem, but it's quite a different story if it's just the pair of them. Our cuddly pets are individuals with feelings. Although I don't know exactly what they feel, their behavior does allow some conjecture. The surviving partner is lethargic and less likely to come trotting up when called. I have the impression that he is mourning or at least misses his partner. What to do? I have no doubt about what must be done in this case. I find him a new partner right away. Of course, you mustn't expect miracles. The two will need time to get used to each other (see Guinea pig companions are important, page 20). Everything is strange for the newcomer, the surroundings as well as the partner. It's easier for the bereaved guinea pig. He just has to get used to the newcomer. I recommend you find a young guinea pig for the one left behind because she will adapt more easily, even if there is a considerable difference in their ages.

Tip: However, there are also other options (see page 20). There's one thing you shouldn't do, though: Don't keep the surviving guinea pig by himself. Of course, you have to bear in mind that

Being alone isn't pleasant for a guinea pig. If one partner dies, the survivor is lonely. ▶

◀ *This tiny bundle of fur is just four days old. She explores her little world inquisitively.*

one animal will eventually be alone again when the older one dies. That's why it's better to keep a small herd right from the start.

When the Cage Is Too Small for the Animals

What exactly does "too small" mean? From the human perspective, this question is difficult to answer. Let's ask the animals. The University of Bern, or, to be precise, the Behavioral Biology Department under the direction of Professor Beat Tschanz, did just that. They compared the behavior of guinea pigs in three different-size cages. The floor space measurements were 24 × 32 inches (60 × 80 cm), 32 × 48 inches (80 × 120 cm), and 48 × 64 inches (120 × 160 cm). All other things, like the number of animals and the cage furnishings, remained the same. The results speak for themselves and reveal a lot about the inner world of the guinea pig.

The small cages have a greater effect on the males than on the females, at least with respect to resting behavior. Males like to go off by themselves and lie down a respectable distance apart. In a small cage, it's impossible for them to get away from each other. As a result, the animals are more aggressive and contact among the males decreases. Guinea pig males are "distance species," as the famous Swiss animal psychologist Professor Heini Hediger discovered. The females, in contrast, are "contact species"; they like to snuggle together. In this respect, the females cope better with a small cage. However, both males

and females are lethargic in small cages. They barely move, have little contact with each other, and show little interest in their surroundings. If you keep guinea pigs in small cages for a long time, they won't bring you very much pleasure. Now a problem arises that has

Guinea pigs need **lots of space**. If the cage is too small, their well-being suffers.

been seen in other animals, too. If the guinea pigs are suddenly offered a larger exercise area or an outdoor pen, they remain crouching apathetically in their little cage.

You have to get animals like this used to the "improved conditions" very slowly. Try to entice the guinea pig out of

The guinea pig can easily be enticed with a tasty dandelion leaf.

▼

the cage with a piece of carrot or some other treat. If necessary, sit down carefully next to the small cage, the animal's familiar surroundings. Lay a trail of food, for instance, pieces of carrot, from the small cage to the large one. If guinea pigs have to live in a cage that is too small, they develop behavioral problems. Guinea pigs don't make it easy for their owner to recognize this. Many other animals show their frustration by harming themselves. They tear out their fur, begin to wreck the cage furnishings, or pace constantly back and forth in the cage. Behavioral biologists call this type of behavior "stereotypy." On very rare occasions I have observed problems like this in guinea pigs kept under bad conditions. They tore out their hair or gnawed on the cage wires. As I said, this is not the norm. Guinea pigs usually seem to suppress their frustration and become lethargic. So don't cut corners in the wrong places; buy a large cage for your guinea pigs right at the start.

When Guinea Pigs Gain Weight Because of Worry

Obesity can have a variety of causes in humans and in animals. On the one hand, genetics plays a role, and on the other, so does the social situation.

Biologist Rüdiger Beer demonstrated most impressively how an unstable social situation affects guinea pigs' appetite. Females that have unfamiliar cage mates every day eat more and gain weight.

This observation was only a small but important part of his research. I find his work exciting. He has made an effort to observe guinea pigs daily throughout their life, record their behavior, test their blood, measure their heart rate, and see how many offspring they have. He compared female herds that always had the same herd members with those that had new herd members every day. Constantly changing the composition of the herd makes the level of stress hormones go up and the heart rate rise. In short, the animals are permanently under stress.

As a result, they eat more. Does that sound familiar?

What's surprising is that, statistically, these females had just as many babies as the females that always lived in the same herd; unfortunately, though, they died one year sooner. Stress, it seems, shortens their life span. Rüdiger Beer

◀ *Children get along beautifully with guinea pigs if their parents teach them how to treat their pets responsibly. This little critter is not at all afraid to let his young owner pick him up.*

summarizes it this way: Live fast, die young.

Tip: Naturally, other common causes of obesity are a cage that is too small, too little out-of-cage time, too little stimulation, and a diet that is too high in calories. Check your animals' living conditions if they are overweight and correct any possible errors in husbandry. Guinea pigs should never go without food. Above all, they need high-fiber foods like hay to maintain intestinal function (see Their ancestors' diet, page 66).

The Guinea Pigs Are Still Shy

It's rare that guinea pigs don't become tame, but it does happen. Check their living conditions. Is the cage in a place where the animals are frightened, or is there a lot of noise that's scaring your guinea pigs? An animal's past history can play a role, too. Some males have more difficulty becoming socialized and therefore have a hard time bonding with humans. In this case, you need patience and more patience. Try to tempt the guinea pigs with treats. In time, they will learn to expect only positive things from you.

The Guinea Pig Has Run Away

Guinea pigs are not escape artists like rabbits. They don't dig and burrow.

··
: **TEST** :
··

Are your animals thriving?

Your guinea pigs' appearance and behavior allow you to gauge quite accurately whether they are doing well.

	Yes	No
1. Do the guinea pigs have contact with others of their kind?	○	○
2. Do the animals often sit together?	○	○
3. Do the guinea pigs communicate with each other using sounds?	○	○
4. Does the guinea pig groom its coat?	○	○
5. Is the guinea pig's coat dense and shiny?	○	○
6. Do the animals spend a lot of time exploring their outdoor pen?	○	○
7. Do they sniff at new objects in the cage?	○	○
8. Do the guinea pigs enjoy having you pet them?	○	○
9. Does their weight remain constant?	○	○
10. Do the guinea pigs try to communicate with you by making noises?	○	○
11. Do your animals make full use of their out-of-cage time?	○	○
12. Do the guinea pigs come running up happily to the side of their cage when you call them?	○	○

ANSWERS: Twelve "yes": Your guinea pigs couldn't be better. They are happy as can be. Nine–eleven "yes": The animals are doing well, but something is troubling them. Find out what it is. Fewer than nine "yes": Improve their living conditions.

Your guinea pigs feel most at home in
familiar surroundings. That's why you should find a
caretaker before you go away on vacation.

Nevertheless, it sometimes happens that one of these little rodents escapes, usually because of the owner's carelessness. This happened to me when I forgot to close the door to the outdoor pen. I searched in vain and had almost given up when I had the following idea: I put a cassette recorder in the pen and played back guinea pig sounds. It was unsuccessful at first—the guinea pig didn't come. Only after I played back the animals' sounds at approximately two-minute intervals did he come running up. I don't know what effect the pauses had, but I would recommend that you make a tape recording of guinea pig sounds—just in case. . . .

The animals need a place to hide when they are afraid.

▼

Vacation and Traveling

Vacation is definitely the nicest time of the year for you and me, but not for most of our pets. Dogs don't mind going along on a vacation trip—the important thing for them is that they're with their master or mistress. It's quite a different story for our guinea pigs. They have to stay home when their owners travel and must adjust accordingly. That's not always easy for the animals and requires careful planning on your part.
Finding a pet-sitter: Start looking around in plenty of time for a reliable person who can take care of your guinea pigs while you're away (see Pet-sitter Checklist, page 136). Guinea pigs feel most comfortable in their familiar surroundings. An unfamiliar environment with strange sounds and smells makes them nervous and fearful. Perhaps you could ask friends or acquaintances to take care of your herd while you're on vacation. Sometimes, though, you're out of luck, and none of your friends has time. I have had good experiences with college students and older children who wanted to earn a little extra money. Posting a notice on the bulletin board at the local university or high school helps in the search.

That's the best option of all. Its main advantage is that everything stays the same, except for the caretaker, and the little critters can easily cope with your temporary absence since, after all, they have each other for company.

Instructing the pet-sitter: Learning by doing applies to your substitute, too. Take your pet-sitter along as you go through your daily routine of guinea pig care. Explain everything in detail, preferably several times. The pet-sitter checklist on page 136 can help your substitute get the hang of caring for your guinea pigs.

What you must avoid: Don't split up the group; otherwise fights can break out later on, especially between male guinea pigs. Don't put your group in

take care of your animals in their familiar surroundings, then some pet dealers, animal shelters, and veterinarians offer pet care services. As mentioned, though, this should be your second choice. Try everything so that your animals can stay in their usual cage or enclosure. This makes the guinea pigs feel safe and secure.

DID YOU KNOW THAT . . .

. . . guinea pigs chatter their teeth?

Teeth chattering or clacking is a threat gesture and can be heard particularly when adult males are about to fight to establish dominance. These sounds are frequently associated with stiffened legs and body. This is how an animal makes himself seem larger to impress another guinea pig. Guinea pigs can also chatter their teeth at you, especially when they're angry at you. That rarely happens, though.

with an unfamiliar guinea pig herd belonging to a friend, because it usually doesn't take long before they're squabbling over pecking order, the males as well as the females. These altercations can be bloody or bloodless. However, even the apparently harmless ones are hard on the animals. The loser sits quietly in a corner and everything seems peaceful. This external peace is deceptive, though. Internally, a flood of stress hormones is unleashed. This stress can quickly lead to the death of the little rodent. If you really can't find anyone to

Improper Treatment

Many times, parents have asked me why their children's guinea pigs immediately run into their house as soon as the children get too close. The explanation is simple: The guinea pigs have had bad experiences with the children. Maybe the children carried them around constantly or handled them too roughly. In a case like this, you and your children should try to find out what's bothering the guinea pigs. Teach the children how to approach the animals carefully and speak to them softly (see page 59 and following). Perhaps the guinea pigs would even let the children tempt them with a treat. Show your children the proper way to pick up and carry the animals (see page 81). It may take quite a while before the animals become trusting again.

Children learn through pets: Pets have a positive influence on children. They demonstrate that animals are thinking, learning, and feeling creatures. Only someone who accepts this can truly understand them and love them properly. This is true for both young and old.

The sooner a person learns about animals, the easier it is to appreciate nature. That is an important goal in the education of our children.

Animals have an almost magical attraction for children, who want to pet them, feed them, play with them, and own them. Nowadays nobody denies the importance of animals for a child's personal development. Research has been done on this topic worldwide.

The answer was always the same. Animals are important for children. Through them, children develop the ability to show consideration and respect for other people. Guinea pigs are ideally suited for this because they usually don't bite and don't pose a danger to children. They are tame and love

1 **How do you teach** your guinea pig to jump over an obstacle? First she must learn to stand up on her hind legs. The best way to do this is with a treat.

2 **When the guinea pig** stands on her hind legs, slowly pull the treat away. The guinea pig will follow the tasty morsel and finally jump over the little hurdle.

Boredom is unhealthy: Little athletic challenges keep them fit. ▶

to be petted and cuddled. Before it gets to this point, though, the children must first learn how to treat their four-legged friends. This is your job as parents: You must teach your children how to care for their pets properly and help them understand the animals. The child must grasp that guinea pigs are sweet but sensitive creatures and that they can't be treated roughly.

When Guinea Pigs Get Old

It is difficult to say how long guinea pigs can live, since the information on age given in the literature varies widely. On average, pet guinea pigs live for six to eight years. The record age is 15 years. For the most part, differences in pet guinea pigs' ages can be traced to the animals' living conditions. Poor conditions shorten their life drastically, because guinea pigs are very susceptible to stress. I know of no other animal in which husbandry conditions are such a good predictor of life expectancy. Guinea pigs live almost twice as long as their relatives the mice (four years), rats (three years), and hamsters (three years). It's still not clear just why this is so. One thing is certain, though: Animals don't live to a ripe old age the way people do. There is no role for grandmoms and granddads as there is with us, where the grandparents help raise the children and pass on important traditions. An animal's life usually ends immediately after the last offspring are born. Its task of ensuring the survival of the species and transmitting its genes has been accomplished.

Signs of old age: Pets usually live longer than their wild cousins. The reason is obvious: In the wild, there is no protection for old and infirm animals. Our pets, on the other hand, are loved and well cared for. No wonder, then, that it's possible to recognize the signs of old age in them after a certain point. The first indications are a dull coat and slight loss of hair. The little critters also become more susceptible to fleas and mites now. Their immune system is probably not working as efficiently as it used to. Minor ailments occur more frequently.

Saying Good-bye

One of our guinea pigs is incurably ill. Our two children (seven and ten years old) don't want us to have the animal put to sleep. Wouldn't a true animal-lover want to free an unfortunate creature like this from its suffering?

You are right. If the veterinarian has told you that there is no hope, then you should have the animal put out of its misery. However, it is important to explain to your children what "true" love of animals means in this case.

Dealing with death

Children usually perceive the death of a pet differently than adults, especially if their animal is to be put to sleep by a veterinarian. They still aren't able to control their feelings, which is not always such a bad thing. The loss of a pet is usually children's first encounter with death and as such is a tremendous shock: Their friend is gone from their life, never to return. With a great deal of sensitivity, you must explain to your children that death is a part of life. Saying good-bye to their four-legged friend will be easier for your children if you explain that animals have no concept of death and therefore no fear of dying. For guinea pigs and other animals, dying is a natural and peaceful process. Try to make this clear to your children.

What happens to the dead animal?

Most children want to bury their four-legged friend. This is perfectly legitimate and helps them cope with their grief. Fortunately, this presents no problem with small animals like guinea pigs. The beloved animal can be buried in the garden, under a bush, or in the lawn. Take your children's grief seriously, even it all seems a bit excessive to you. Make a little "coffin" for the animal, perhaps from a shoe box. Incidentally, you can buy genuine little wooden caskets at the pet store. You don't have to go to this extreme, though. In my opinion, a simple cardboard box works just as well. Lay the little body in it and decorate the "final resting place" with a few leaves and flowers. Enclose the body or box in a plastic bag to reduce the chance of your friend being dug up by a pet or wild animal.

Burying Your Guinea Pig

I know it sounds sentimental, but you can have a little funeral for your children's best friend. If possible, mark the grave with a wooden cross or a stone on which you've written the animal's name. A grave like this is often very comforting for children.

What to watch out for now: Make sure that the animal is getting enough vitamins and minerals. Other than that, stick to the usual menu. Although older guinea pigs become quieter and like a little nap in the sun, they are at no disadvantage in the group. They are neither pushed away from the food nor expelled from the herd. Old and young get along well together. They are still surprisingly fit mentally. As we discovered, even older animals were able to learn new tricks, and they didn't forget tasks that they had learned a year before. Their memory functions well. In older guinea pigs, as with many mammals, the heart rate increases and the eyes become cloudy and lose fluid. This fluid loss causes a change in intraocular pressure. It's still not known if this results in any noticeable changes in vision. Guinea pigs probably suffer some hearing loss, because they squeal, purr, gurgle, and call less often. No one knows exactly. The same is true of the other sensory organs. It may comfort you to know that all these aging processes begin late and then progress quickly.

When guinea pigs die

Dying appears to be easy and peaceful, and it takes only a few minutes. I have never observed a "death struggle" like that seen in some people. Everything that I know about how our little friends die is based on my own observations. As far as I know, no research has been done on this subject. Most of my animals ate less on the day they died and barely moved, and a few stayed inside their nest box. They probably just wanted to go off by themselves. With the others, I could see exactly how they died. The animal lay on its side, just as it did when going to sleep. It remained in this position, dozing and breathing heavily. Suddenly its body twitched several times, and the little creature was dead.

Two good friends ▶
share everything:
This guinea pig
has come to
inspect his
friend's new
home.

MY PET

How do guinea pigs spend their day?

Become a behavioral scientist for a day and find out how your guinea pigs spend their time. Determine whether the animals rest or are active at certain times and when they are especially sociable.

The test begins:

Note down the behavior of one guinea pig at six different times over the course of the day for fifteen minutes at a time. Limit yourself to one animal; it's too difficult to observe several animals at the same time. Write down everything your animal does. It's even better to film the behavior with a video camera. If you enjoy doing this, you can continue your research for a few more days.

My test results:

The herd mates: They scarcely reacted to their dead companion. That surprised me, so I left the little corpse in the cage for a few hours. The only thing I was able to discover was that they sniffed at the dead animal briefly. Not a trace of grief was apparent. It's difficult to judge what really goes on in their minds. I suspect that they no longer regarded the dead herd member as one of their own.

Tip: Fortunately, guinea pigs don't suffer when they die, and you don't need to have them euthanized by a veterinarian. However, in case of a severe and painful illness, you should not hesitate to have the veterinarian put an end to the animal's suffering with an injection.

If a guinea pig is challenged physi- ▶
cally and mentally, she will not have
any behavioral problems.

Pet-sitter Checklist

Would you like to take a vacation and have a sitter look after your pets? Here you can write down everything that your substitute should know while you're on vacation. This way your guinea pigs will receive the best of care and you can enjoy your trip.

These are my guinea pigs' names:

This is what they look like:

This is what they like to eat:

This amount daily:

This amount once a week:

Between-meal snacks:

This is what they drink:

This is when to feed them:

The food is stored here:

Housekeeping:

This is cleaned every day:

This is cleaned once a week:

They like to be petted like this:

Great activities for them:

They really dislike this:

What my animals are not allowed to do:

This is especially important:

This is their veterinarian's name:

My address and telephone number while I'm on vacation:

INDEX

ADDRESSES/ LITERATURE

ADDRESSES OF CLUBS AND ORGANIZATIONS

American Cavy Breeders Association
16540 Hogan Avenue
Hastings, MN 55033
www.acbaonline.com

American Rabbit Breeders Association (national organization for domestic rabbit and cavy breeders)
P.O. Box 426
Bloomington, IL 61702
www.arba.net

BOOKS

Vanderlip, Sharon L., D.V.M. 2003. *The Guinea Pig Handbook.* Hauppauge, NY: Barron's Educational Series

Birmelin, Immanuel. 2001. *My Guinea Pig and Me.* Hauppauge, NY: Barron's Educational Series

Behrend, Katrin. 1998. *Guinea Pigs (A Complete Pet Owner's Manual).* Hauppauge, NY: Barron's Educational Series

Behrend, Katrin. 1997. *The Guinea Pig.* Hauppauge, NY: Barron's Educational Series

Sachser, Norbert, Christine Künzel, and Sylvia Kaiser. 2004. "The Welfare of Laboratory Guinea Pigs" in Kalista, E. (ed.) *The Welfare of Laboratory Animals.* Dordrecht, Netherlands: Kluver Academic Publishers.

MAGAZINES

Critters USA.
P.O. Box 6050
Mission Viejo, CA 92690
www.animalnetwork.com

USEFUL WEBSITES

(These contain information on care, housing, health, poisonous plants, pet-sitters, and links to other guinea pig sites)

"Cavy Care Site"
www.geocities.com/
Heartland/Plains/2517

"Seagull's Guinea Pig Compendium"
www.aracnet.com/~seagull/
Guineas/

Information on medical care:

"Free Animal Health Resources from the College of Veterinary Medicine at Cornell University"
www.vet.cornell.edu/library/
freeresources.htm

"Guinea Lynx: A Medical and Care Guide for Your Guinea Pig"
www.guinealynx.com

"VeterinaryPartner" (information on health care)
www.veterinarypartner.com

Information on poisonous plants:

"Cornell University Poisonous Plants Informational Database"
www.ansci.cornell.edu/
plants/index.html

"Poisonous Plants" (University of Pennsylvania School of Veterinary Medicine)
http://cal.vet.upenn.edu/
poison

Information on pet-sitters:

"National Association of Professional Pet Sitters"
www.petsitters.org

"Pet Sitters International"
www.petsit.com

ACKNOWLEDG-MENTS

I would like to thank Professor Norbert Sachser and his team, who have contributed significantly to our understanding of the guinea pig. I would also like to thank my doctoral adviser, Professor Beat Tschanz, who introduced me to behavioral biology.

THE PHOTOS

The photographs on the introductory page of each chapter illustrate the following:

Page 6: Guinea pigs don't guard their food jealously. They're usually happy to share and share alike.

Page 32: A hiding place is especially important for a flight animal like the guinea pig. Wooden hide boxes with two entrances are highly recommended.

Page 50: Who wouldn't like to have a friendly guinea pig? Cultivate their trust right from the start; then nothing can go wrong.

Page 64: A tasty veggie kabob like this will keep your guinea pigs busy for a long time.

Page 78: Nap time—who dares to disturb us? It is important to respect the animals' rest periods.

Page 96: Activity is essential for mental and physical health.

Page 105: Mother and pup. The little ones are independent at an early age.

Page 122: A new companion moves in. Acclimation must proceed very gently.

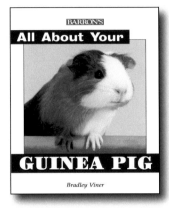
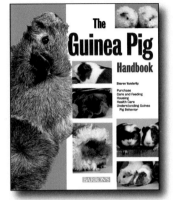

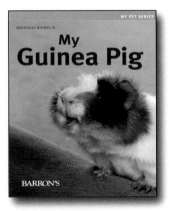

The Author

Behavioral biologist Dr. Immanuel Birmelin of Freiburg, Germany, has spent the past 25 years studying the behavior of domestic animals as well as animals in zoos and circuses. His own menagerie includes guinea pigs, parakeets, and dogs. Barron's Educational Series has published several of Professor Birmelin's books: *Budgerigars, My Parakeet and Me, My Guinea Pig and Me,* and *The New Parakeet Handbook.* In addition, the author is a scientific adviser for wildlife films and an expert on animal husbandry.

The Photographer

Oliver Giel specializes in animal and nature photography. His photos appear in many magazines and pet-care handbooks. All photos in this book are his with the following exceptions: Toni Angermayer: pages 8, 9-1, 9-2; Artemis View/Elsner: pages 29 top right; Regina Kuhn: page 26 top, 26 bottom; Ulrike Schanz: page 27 top right, 30 top right, 30 bottom right, 31 top, 31 bottom left, 31 bottom right.

First edition for the United States, its territories and dependencies, and Canada published in 2008 by Barron's Educational Series, Inc.

Published originally under the title *mein Meerschweinchen,* in the series *mein Heimtier*
© 2006 by Gräfe and Unzer Verlag GmbH, München

G|U

English translation © Copyright 2008 by Barron's Educational Series, Inc.
German edition by: Immanuel Birmelin

English translation by Mary D. Lynch

All inquiries should be addressed to:
Barron's Educational Series, Inc.
250 Wireless Boulevard
Hauppauge, New York 11788
www.barronseduc.com

Library of Congress Cataloging-in-Publication Data

Birmelin, I. (Immanuel)
  [Mein Meerschweinchen. English]
  My guinea pig / Immanuel Birmelin.
    p. cm. — (My pet)
  Includes bibliographical references and index.
  ISBN-13: 978-0-7641-3799-0 (alk. paper)
  ISBN-10: 0-7641-3799-9 (alk. paper)
  1. Guinea pigs as pets. I. Title
  SF459.G9B55513 2008
  636.935'92—dc22

                                           2007037229

ISBN-13: 978-0-7641-3799-0
ISBN-10: 0-7641-3799-9

Printed in China

9 8

NOTE

Some skin diseases affecting guinea pigs can be transmitted to humans. If you suspect you have been infected, see your physician. Some people have an allergic reaction to animal hair. Consult your physician before buying a guinea pig.